To Sean /sarah.
from Dad,

THE '80s KID

ANDREW MURRAY

KNOCK KNOCK, OPEN WIDE,
SEE WHAT'S ON THE OTHER SIDE.

**DEDICATED TO
GRANDDAD, PAULINE AND CLAIRE**

▶ ▶ ▶

FIRST PUBLISHED 2011
SALTWATER PUBLISHING LTD
119 LOWER BAGGOT STREET
DUBLIN 2, IRELAND
WWW.SALTWATER.IE

BRITISH LIBRARY CATALOGUING IN
PUBLICATION DATA. A CATALOGUE RECORD
FOR THIS BOOK IS AVAILABLE FROM THE
BRITISH LIBRARY.ISBN 978-1-908366-03-0

PRINTED AND BOUND IN SINGAPORE
DESIGNED BY RED&GREY DESIGN
WWW.REDANDGREYDESIGN.IE

  **Red&Grey
Design**

Saltwater

CONTENTS

▶ ▶ ▶

FOREWORD

▶ ▶ ▶

BY DERMOT WHELAN

'DERMOT, DID
YOUR MOTHER
CUT YOUR HAIR?'

IT WAS COUNTY LIMERICK IN 1981 AND
THE QUESTION CAME FROM MY NEXT-DOOR
NEIGHBOUR AFTER I CHARGED IN HER BACK
DOOR. I WAS EIGHT YEARS OLD, ON MY WAY
TO HER SON'S CUPBOARD TO PLAY WITH HIS
LEGO. I KNEW HE WASN'T THERE, I JUST
WANTED TO PLAY WITH HIS LEGO.

'YES,' I REPLIED, THINKING THAT
IT WAS A SILLY QUESTION. WHO ELSE
WAS GOING TO CUT IT?

'IT LOOKS … GREAT.
DID SHE HAVE TO GO OUT?'

'YES, SHE WENT TO THE SHOPS FOR
MESSAGES,' I SAID, WONDERING HOW
SHE KNEW. MUST BE A MAMMY THING.
I DISAPPEARED INTO THE BOWELS OF THE
BUNGALOW. OF COURSE, MRS WYLIE KNEW
MY MOTHER HAD TO GO OUT IN A RUSH
BECAUSE SHE HAD ONLY CUT THE HAIR ON
ONE SIDE OF MY HEAD. I LOOKED LIKE
MY OWN 'BEFORE AND AFTER' PICTURE.
SYMMETRY WAS CLEARLY NOT IMPORTANT TO
MY MOTHER WHEN THERE WERE YELLOW PACK
TINNED PEACHES TO BE BOUGHT. I DIDN'T
CARE. I WAS TOO BUSY ATTACHING THE LEGO
HEAD OF A RED INDIAN TO THE DASHBOARD
OF A BROKEN STARSHIP.

BECAUSE THAT'S WHAT THE '80S
WERE. AN EXCITING AND LIMITLESS
WORLD OF BROKEN BUCKAROOS, FIZZ
BOMBS, LONG EVENINGS, PUSH STARTS,
GAY BYRNE, BIG TRAK (YES, I WAS
PRIVILEGED) ACTION MAN'S HANDS,
GOLF-BALL CHEWING GUMS, GLENROE,
BMX ACCIDENTS, 2P'S, SOLDIERS
STUCK TO BARE FEET, ANGEL DELIGHT,
RUBIX CUBES, ENDLESS SUMMERS AND
MR FREEZES, ALL ACCOMPANIED BY
A REASSURING SOUNDTRACK OF RED
LEMONADE BURPS AND THE SCREECH OF
A ZX SPECTRUM GAME ATTEMPTING TO
LOAD BUT NEVER QUITE SUCCEEDING.

THANK YOU, ANDREW, FOR THIS BOOK.
BECAUSE THIS IS NOT JUST A BOOK.
IT IS AN HISTORICAL RECORD. LIKE
THUCYDIDES OF ANCIENT GREECE AND
TACITUS OF ROME, ANDREW WAS CHOSEN
BY THE GODS TO DOCUMENT THIS PIVOTAL
TIME IN HISTORY - THE GREAT 1980S.
LEST ANYONE FORGET THAT CHILDREN
ROAMED THE STREETS WITH HALF A
HAIRCUT OR THAT PUTTING MILK IN
A SODASTREAM WILL NEVER END WELL …

INTRODUCTION ▶▶▶

THIS BOOK IS AN UNASHAMEDLY ROSE-TINTED TAKE ON GROWING UP IN '80S IRELAND, TOLD THROUGH THE EYES OF BARRY, ANNE, JOHN PAUL AND THE AUTHOR.

BARRY (BORN 1978)

NICE GUY, BUT HIS WEAKNESS IS THE LADIES. WENT TO LOCAL CBS AND SHIFTED FIRST GIRL TO BRYAN ADAMS' (EVERYTHING I DO) I DO IT FOR YOU' AFTER SNEAKING INTO A TEENAGE DISCO IN 1991. HE HOLIDAYED IN THE NICER PARTS OF LEINSTER AND KERRY WITH THE FAMILY AND TORMENTED THE GIRLS IN THE EVENING DISCOS IN THE GAELTEACHT. HE IS NOW AN ACCOUNTANT AND IS MARRIED WITH TWO KIDS. HE DID WELL IN THE BOOM YEARS AND HE REMORTGAGED HIS REMORTGAGED HOUSE, LIKE HIS BUDDIES, AND ENDED UP WITH THREE PROPERTIES: THE FAMILY HOME THAT IS NOW WORTH 25 PER CENT OF THE PRICE HE PAID FOR IT, AN INVESTMENT APARTMENT IN A 'NEW TOWN' IN LONG-RANGE COMMUTERVILLE THAT HAS BEEN VACANT SINCE COMPLETION IN 2009 AND A HALF-BUILT HOLIDAY HOME IN BULGARIA. HE HAS JUST RECEIVED HIS THIRD PAY CUT IN FOUR YEARS AND THE EXTRAVAGANT LIFESTYLE HAS GONE, PUTTING HIS MARRIAGE UNDER STRAIN.

ANNE (BORN 1974, ALLEGEDLY)

NICE GIRL, BUT HER WEAKNESS IS CHARDONNAY AND TRUSTING PEOPLE A BIT TOO MUCH. WENT TO THE LOCAL CONVENT SCHOOL AND IS AN ALL-ROUND GOOD GIRL. HOWEVER, SHE SOWED THE WILD OATS WHEN SHE DID INTERMEDIATE BOOKKEEPING AT A REGIONAL TECHNICAL COLLEGE, AND AGAIN WHEN SHE WAS TWENTY-THREE ON A 'MAD' CLUB 18-30 HOLIDAY IN CORFU (SHE DIDN'T EVEN WANT TO GO, YET SHE WAS THE WORST/BEST OF THE EIGHT GIRLS AND ENDED UP 1ST ON THE LEADERBOARD WITH 8 FROM 7). SHE LIVES ALONE AND DRINKS A BOTTLE OF WINE A NIGHT, BUT ONLY SMOKES ON NIGHTS OUT. SHE HAS NEVER REALLY LET GO OF HER YOUTH.

JOHN PAUL (BORN 1982)

LITTLE FECKER WITH NO WEAKNESSES. LEFT SCHOOL AT SIXTEEN. HE HOLIDAYED IN MOSNEY AND COURTOWN, AND SPENT MANY WEEKS IN EXILE IN HIS COUSINS' HOUSES IN THE MIDLANDS WHEN HIS PARENTS GOT SICK OF HIM. DURING HIS TEENS, HE COULD BE FOUND SELLING FIREWORKS ON MOORE STREET FROM JUNE TO NOVEMBER. HE NOW DRIVES A TAXI AND WORKS AS A BOUNCER AT A WELL-KNOWN LATE-NIGHT DRINKING ESTABLISHMENT IN DUBLIN 2. HE WOULD NOT CHANGE A THING ABOUT HIS CHILDHOOD.

CHARACTERS IN BOOK = COLOURED ICONS

KNOCK KNOCK, ANY MORE, COME WITH ME THROUGH THE MAGIC DOOR ...

CHAPTER 1

THE SUMMERS

At the gang's first general assembly of the holidays the main call of business was to plan the summer goings on in minute detail. Two or three glorious months lay out in front of us to do nothing but play, watch TV, head off on holiday, hang out and get up to mischief.

Young boys would plan how they were going to build that base beside the river, while the older lads would discuss how they were going to impress the gamey Anne Marie and her mates. Young girls addressed the pressing issue of whether dolls would be granted entry to their Teddy Bear's picnic, while the older girls thrashed out whose hair would be first to get the 'Sun-In' treatment.

The summers stretched out so far in front of you when you got your holidays but September seemed to come around painfully quickly. There were no complaints about 'no facilities'; you would look for things to do, and invariably you would find them! Adventures, feelings of unparalleled happiness, bouts of boredom, love stories, games, and mishaps were all part of the joy of the summer holidays.

79% OF '80S KIDS SURVEYED, FOR WHATEVER REASON, RECKONED THAT THEY HAVE NOT SEEN WHITE DOG POO ON THE STREET DURING THE SUMMERS SINCE THE BEGINNING OF THE '90S.

GET OUTSIDE

My mother and most people's parents didn't really like us back then. I remember as soon as you got the summer holidays from school, the very next morning you would get kicked out of the house because 'the weather is too good for you to be stuck inside watching that bleedin' box'. You would dip a toe outside and the wind and rain would nearly cut you in two, before the push in the back and the shout of 'don't come back here until you're called'. And as for sun cream? I had never heard of it.

34% OF '80S BOYS AND GIRLS COULD NOT REMEMBER USING SUN CREAM AS A CHILD.

FACT

Having thousands of midge(t) bites at the end of every single day. If you were sent to go and help some auld fecker on his farm somewhere up the road, you would end up with millions of bites.

The smell of freshly cut grass on a sunny summer morning was wonderful, as the girls and myself had a picnic and played dolls on blankets before shrewdly putting our money together to buy food for the whole gang.

GRASS

MIDGETS

Catching bees in jars while we were meant to be collecting blackberries.

Dad was the hero and you copied absolutely everything he did. I loved heading off with Dad to catch tadpoles, and then trying to grow the tadpoles into frogs in the back garden.

WHEN WE SET THE WHEELS IN MOTION FOR THE BIGGEST NIGHT OF THE YEAR – HALLOWEEN. THE COLLECTING FOR THE BONFIRE WOULD START IN THE SUMMER AND WE WOULD RAID THE LOCAL SUPERMARKETS, FURNITURE STORES AND GARAGES FOR THE HOLY GRAILS OF PALLETS AND TYRES.

TOP TIPS

THROW A SLICE OF STRAWBERRY INTO A POND TO HELP CATCH TADPOLES.

BURN BABY BURN

TADPOLES

9

THE GRAVE SNATCHER

Heading to the graveyard beside where we lived, before coming home in the evening with a bunch of stolen flowers to Mum. All would be right in the world until she went out for a Saturday shopping trip in town with her sister. On her return she would find the house fairly empty after you had sold half the contents of the house on the road doing your sale of work.

Mrs O'Reilly:
How much for the crystal clock, love?

Me:
Is 15p okay, Mrs O'Reilly?

Perfume de Cabinet de Liqueur

Mesdemoiselles

Go to the parents' drinks cabinet and take some of their vodka. Then go outside and pluck all the rose petals off your neighbour's bush. Place the petals into a bowl with the vodka and crush the petals. And 'hey presto', you have perfume.

Au revoir

GHETTO BLASTER

walking through the estate to the shop with the top off and a ghetto blaster on my shoulder to hang around and wait to smoke the butts that people would drop.

Gold

♥

Summer afternoons were spent making perfume from rose petals to sell door to door, making lemonade and selling it on the street, and putting on variety shows for the neighbourhood and charging other kids a jelly to watch. Sir Alan or Bill would have been proud of us!

THE TAR ON THE ROAD IN THE ESTATES MELTING FROM THE HEAT (THE SUMMERS FELT HOTTER IN THE '80s) AND IT STICKING TO YOUR RUNNERS, AND THEN YOUR MAM GOING NUTS.

LEGGER

During the boredom of the summer we would just do things to get a chase. There is no better feeling in the world than running until you are out of breath. Where I was brought up, the chase was usually from a neighbour, security man, a caretaker or the gardaí.

99

Mr Whippy

Having an ice-cream cone with everything on it on a warm afternoon from our local ice-cream van that played the usual Music-Box-Dancer tune when it was moving, but belted out Elvis tunes when it stopped. 'Mr Perfect', as my Mum used to say, was our ice-cream man and all the mothers in the neighbourhood would put make-up on before asking for a screwball.

FACT

7% OF '80S BOYS AND GIRLS SURVEYED DID NOT TELL THEIR PARENTS THAT THERE WAS A CHEWING GUM IN THE END OF A SCREWBALL.

BEEP **BEEP**
BEEP BEEP

GANGSTERS AROUND THE GLOBE HAVE 'PLAYED DEAD' TO STEAL PEOPLE'S CARS.

Another long summer evening activity was 'playing dead'. we had a quiet-ish main road running along the edge of where we lived. A gang of us would hide behind a wall to wait until no cars were coming along the road. Then one of us, usually me, would jump the wall and lie down at the side of the road with the eyes closed.

The best, or worst depending on how you look at it, one ever was when a young Lady driver passes by me before coming to a screeching stop. she jumps from the car and runs towards me screaming. As soon as she gets to me, I jump up and start running, as do all the gang from behind the wall. Terrible stuff really ....

MAKING HAY

The cornfields at the edge of the estate would be cut and baled. we would all watch and pray that it would be the 'round ones'. once you saw that first bale drop and it was round, we knew that it was going to be a good week. The round bales could be rolled together to make a base, could be rolled into ditches, or strategically rolled onto main roads to annoy drivers. If the farmer decided on 'square ones', we only cut all the strings and burned them.

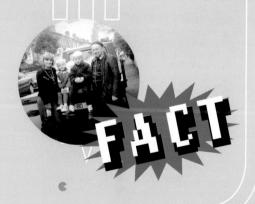

Getting a jaunt on the back of the coal lorry and milk van when they came on the road.

THE TERM 'GETTING A JAUNT' IN CERTAIN WESTERN COUNTIES, IS SLANG FOR HAVING A NAKED LIE-DOWN CUDDLE WITH SOMEONE.

THE AIM BACK THEN FOR ME WAS TO SET FIRE TO ABSOLUTELY
EVERYTHING. IT STARTED WHEN I GOT A MAGNIFYING GLASS
FOR THE 5TH BIRTHDAY. FIRST, IT WAS JUST SIMPLE
THINGS LIKE LEAVES, PAPER AND GRILLING A FEW WORMS
BEFORE FORCE-FEEDING THEM TO THE YOUNGER COUSINS.
IT SWIFTLY MOVED ON WHEN I GOT MY HANDS ON A BOX
OF MATCHES FOR THE FIRST TIME. TREES, PEOPLE'S
RUBBISH BINS AND GERALD'S NEW LA GEAR RUNNERS
ALL GOT IT. THEN WHEN I GOT A LIGHTER, I WOULD
HAVE GREAT FUN COVERING ABSOLUTELY EVERYTHING
IN 'MICKEY DROPS'. THIS INVOLVED SETTING
FIRE TO A PLASTIC BAG AND THEN RUNNING
AROUND DROPPING BURNING MOLTEN PLASTIC
ON EVERY SURFACE IN SIGHT.

Image: Laura Bell

FACT!

*6% OF '80S
BOYS AND GIRLS
REALLY LIKED
TO BURN THINGS.*

*THE US ARMY DID NOT INVENT
WATERBOARDING AS A TORTURE
TECHNIQUE. IT WAS INVENTED
IN THE SUMMER OF '87 IN
SUBURBAN DUBLIN AS A SURE-
FIRE METHOD OF OBTAINING
NOT JUST THE LETTER BUT THE
ENTIRE WORD IN THE GAME
'BASH THE LETTER' OR 'BASH
'EM IRA'. PLEASE REFER TO THE
GAMES CHAPTER FOR A MORE
DETAILED DESCRIPTION.*

Image: Rod Z

One person in the neighbourhood
would get a Super Soaker and before
the week was out, everyone in the
area would have one. Water fights
were not water fights, they were
all-out war.

FACT!

By 1990, the violence had escalated
from water guns to highly dangerous
homemade weapons which included
bottles, buckets and dogbaths.

GOING TO THE
CINEMA DURING THE
WEEK WITH THE GANG
AND PAYING INTO ONE
FILM (IF WE HAD TO)
AND WHEN IT FINISHED
GOING INTO ALL THE
OTHER FILMS FOR THE
REST OF THE DAY.

On the long summer days I would have three or four 'best' friends one day, and the next day, one or two would be replaced with someone else (because it was her birthday the following week and her Dad was bringing everyone to McDonald's). We were quite the social butterflies.

♥

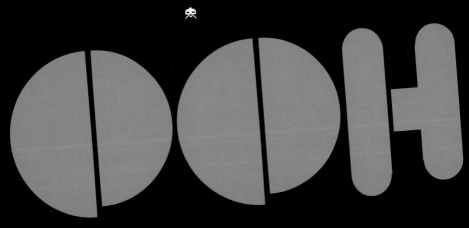

Whatever big sporting event was on during the summer, it would be copied on the street. Football was always played, but during Euro '88 and Italia '90, even the boys who preferred skateboarding and grunge, the boys who preferred to hang out with the girls singing and playing dolls, and the boys that liked Star Trek and Ataris were found out on the green pretending to be Whelan, Aldridge or Houghton.

IRELAND

RONNIE WHELAN

I remember playing football on the green from morning until evening and getting so hot that you would sip the rainwater off railings, gates and car windows.

CASIO WATCH

The Olympics were also massive. There would be arguments over who was either Coe or Ovett in '80 and Ben Johnson or Carl Lewis in '88. An adapted neighbourhood Decathlon event was held after Daley Thompson's win in '80 and '84, with boys and girls competing in events such as: how many of the younger kids can you hit with a marble in one minute (timed on your Casio watch), how quickly can you climb the chestnut tree, and how fast you can run through the lane full of nettles (disqualification would occur if you needed a doc leaf), to name just three.

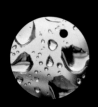

TOP TIPS

INSTEAD OF SPITTING ON A DOC LEAF, URINATE ON IT BEFORE RUBBING IT ON A FRIEND'S LEG/ARM AFTER A NETTLE STING. PLEASE NOTE THAT THIS HAS NO ADDITIONAL MEDICINAL BENEFIT.

OUT

The big annual sporting event of 'Street Tennis' took place during the two weeks of Wimbledon in June.

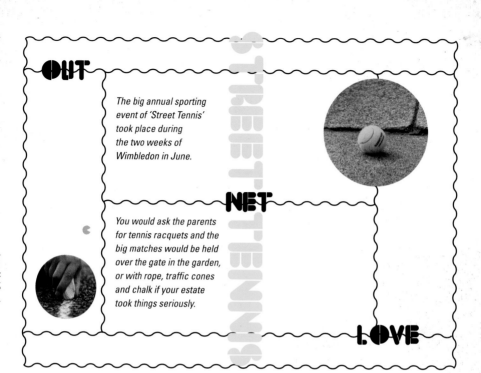

NET

You would ask the parents for tennis racquets and the big matches would be held over the gate in the garden, or with rope, traffic cones and chalk if your estate took things seriously.

Image: Mark Cacovic

LOVE

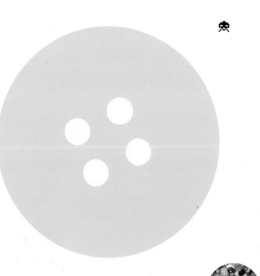

Also, we would have a running battle every summer with the next estate or town (War of the Buttons had nothing on it). In the film, after capturing one of the enemy, Little Con shouts 'His willie, cut off his willie ….'. There is a rumour that one of the older lads from the estate, Rubber Murphy, did actually cut off Redzer Bennett's 'little man'. True or not, I don't know.

WAR

When around the corner seemed far away,
the next estate seemed like a different county
and going up to Dublin for the day seemed like
going to a different country! I would regularly
travel to Dublin with Mum for a day's shopping
and 'rooting' in Frawley's and Guineys. I also
remember being scared of the mad auld one (Mad
Mary) who used to dance on O'Connell Street.

♥

RUBBER DUCKY
YOU AND ME
AND MY SISTER

You and your brother
or sister having a bath
after a long hard day
playing, to avoid running
the bath twice.

The parents sending you to your relations in the midlands to 'help out' in the bog. I don't think it is an exaggeration to say that kids in concentration camps or kids currently making runners in Vietnam have easier weeks than this week of intense labour during every summer of my youth. In fairness, we did get to go home after a week, concentration camp and 'runner' kids do not, unfortunately!

Image: Paddy (scrawb)

OULT RIDER

When I was seven, uncle Austin would have me up at 6am. You would make the trip to the bog on the cart after a big bowl of porridge. The uncles and other auld fellas would cut new turf, while all us young lads would turn the sods and foot the ones that were ready from a week or two earlier. We would then make stacks and fill the fertiliser bags from the turf that had been there a few weeks – pure back-breaking stuff. You got two half-hour breaks to eat your corn-beef sambos that your aunt had made, along with a Thermos of tea. Every time tea was needed, you would have to go to retrieve the bottles of milk that you had thrown into a boghole to keep them cool for the day. After more slavish work, you would leave at 5pm to head home for dinner, to pray that Tuesday, Wednesday, Thursday and Friday go quickly. You would then arrive back home to Mam and Dad on Friday evening looking like Quasimodo.

Heading off to visit the Grandparents who lived 'in the country', 10 miles up the road. For some reason, when you were five or six, it felt like going away on holiday every second or third day, and you would have a new garden to explore. A Granddad's back garden in the '80s would contain bits of everything, and he would have a shed full of auld scrap that you would love to mess with.

I was banished to the aunts and uncles in the midlands too a couple of times every summer, when the mother was sick of me in a type of 'cousin swap'. These trips would help me calm down and got me off the drink and smokes for a few weeks when I was 11. I can't even remember the places where the relations lived. sure all of those counties are the same, are they not? - Longford, offaly, westmeath, Roscommon.

BANISHED

OH B'GORRAH!

A HOLIDAY GUIDE TO

IReLAND

Danger

The North
DANGER

NO
DANGER

The Wesht Coast
Gaeltacht

The Midlands
Nutjob Land

● Mosney
● Bettystown

The Eastcoast

Skerries
Dublin
● Bray

● Brittas

● Courtown

Cork
The Pretend
Capital

**Sellafieldal
Drift**

Basic Guide to Irishness

The
North

The
Country**

Dublin*

Cork
People***

Nordies

Dublin

Culchies

* Dublin is in fact the capital of Ireland. Dubliners rarely brag about this or think they are superior. Dublin therefore is considered the main focal point of Ireland. This means any place outside here is 'the country' i.e not the city. Leaving the 'city' meant leaving civilisation.

** Most culchies resent being called culchies as it implies an interest in farming/paganism/Gaelic. Certain jokes like: 'Do you have electricity in …?' or 'Do you have television in …?' are also associated with this implication.

*** For some reason Cork people think Cork is the capital.

**Foreign Soil
/ Fancy Posh Holidays**

The field trip day in the Summer Projects was always great. Usually to a playground and once a summer to an adventure centre. Playing in the coloured balls was my thing. I could stay there all day.

FACT

41% OF '80S BOYS AND GIRLS SURVEYED SHIFTED MORE THAN 5 MEMBERS OF THE OPPOSITE SEX IN A SINGLE NIGHT AT A TEENAGE DISCO ON MORE THAN ONE OCCASION.

GAELTACHT

Pretending to be really interested in mastering Irish as a teenager to persuade your parents to send you to the Gaeltacht for 3 weeks to 'immerse yourself in the language'. Everyone knows the real reason we wanted to go was to shift absolutely anything that moved at the céilís every evening. Trying to shift girls took up a huge portion of the teenage years. A fantastic time in the neighbourhood was when the extended cousins of friends and other people from the estate would arrive over to a birthday party.

The smell of 'fresh shifting meat' would infiltrate the senses and the posse would congregate in the front garden of the birthday party to chance the arm. This in-built desire to shift anything probably stemmed from our parents, uncles and aunts asking us to kiss any doll in the room when we were toddlers, this is my theory anyway!

FACT

66% OF
'80S BOYS & GIRLS
WOULD BRING THEIR
KIDS TO MOSNEY
IF IT WAS
REOPENED.

Dad packing the car and filling the roof rack for the big trip somewhere, usually to a caravan (Mam always told us to tell everyone that we were going to a mobile home) in Wexford. The best part of the week was the journey, as we would stop in the Dún Laoghaire Baths 'Rainbow Rapids'. This place was brilliant and I would love to bring the kids to it, but unfortunately it is in ruins now. Anyway, we would get to Wexford and the whole trip involved playing patience/solitaire while waiting for the rain to clear (it never really cleared) and Dad drink driving home each night.

MOSNEY

HEADING OFF TO MOSNEY WITH THE MOTHER, HER FRIEND, THE FRIEND'S KIDS AND A BABYSITTER FOR A WEEK. ACTIVITIES DURING THE DAY FOR ME INCLUDED:

sinking swan pedalos on the lake.

shaking the slot machines that you would drop a coin down to move other coins and 'winning money'.

Being made to get up and sing 'The Green Fields of France' at kid talent shows.

Getting kicked out of the pool for too much petting of a young one under the mushrooms.

Getting kicked out of the pool for jumping head first down the coca cola slide.

Getting kicked out of the pool for standing in my speedos and mooning through the big glass panes at parents enjoying the entertainment in Dan Lowery's.

Getting kicked out of the pool for pushing a shite out in front of big glass panes at parents enjoying the entertainment in Dan Lowery's.

ACTIVITIES DURING THE NIGHT FOR ME INCLUDED:

wrecking the babysitter's head.

Doing Niknaks/Nick Nocks.

Trying to get the babysitter to play spin the bottle.

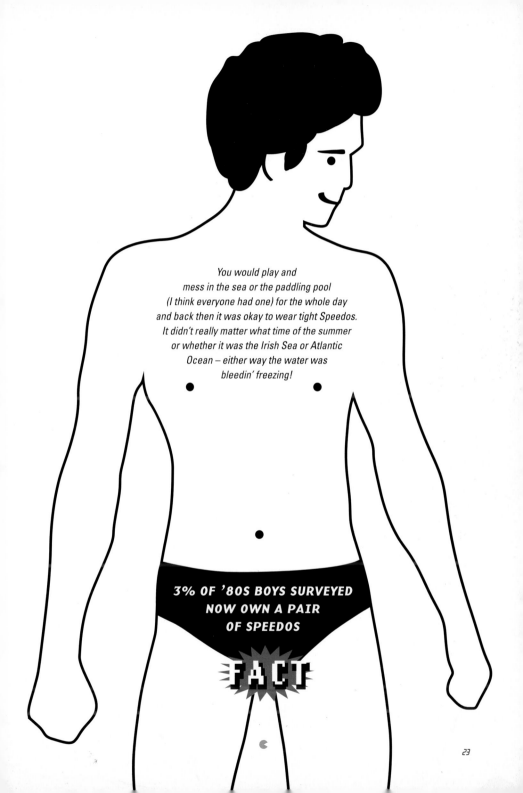

You would play and
mess in the sea or the paddling pool
(I think everyone had one) for the whole day
and back then it was okay to wear tight Speedos.
It didn't really matter what time of the summer
or whether it was the Irish Sea or Atlantic
Ocean – either way the water was
bleedin' freezing!

**3% OF '80S BOYS SURVEYED
NOW OWN A PAIR
OF SPEEDOS**

FACT

Going on the big trip to the coast for the summer. You could not wait to get there and into your little pink swimsuit. Then the reality would set in as you got to the beach. 90% of the time was spent lying down, covering yourself with lots of towels behind a windbreaker because it was feckin' freezing. When the sun did fall through the clouds and the gale abated for 3 minutes in every 4 hours, you would run to the sea and stand at its edge, sinking into the quicksand. Then you would run in and jump waves before they would finally knock you down.

FACT

You would see a boy on your holidays and you thought that by talking to him, it meant it was love. You would give him a jelly ring or a Hula Hoop, and that sealed it, you were engaged and would be married.

74% OF '80S BOYS AND GIRLS WERE IN LOVE AND GOING OUT WITH SOMEONE DURING A SUMMER, YET NEVER EVEN SHARED A KISS.

other than Mosney, and when I was sent to the aunts in Cavan or someplace, all I remember is riding a smelly donkey on a beach somewhere in coastal culchieland. I think it was Bray or somewhere stupid like that, where even I had trouble trying to 'outmad' the locals.

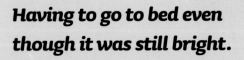

Having to go to bed even though it was still bright.

CHAPTER 2

THE GAMES

When we were kids, any minute that we didn't have to be at school or in Mass was spent outside playing. We had some seriously amazing games in the '80s. Without fail, just as a game was reaching a climax that seemed more epic to us than a World Cup final, someone would be called in for their dinner. A certain game would be flavour of the month until a local kid got back from a weekend in their cousin's town where they'd learnt a 'new' game that would soon get its fifteen minutes of fame.

Some games were harmless and fun and everyone would enjoy them, others involved a certain amount of pressure and a lot of partakers partook only reluctantly, while others were pure and unadulterated evil and involved inflicting physical and mental harm on other children. There are thousands of games to choose from. Here are some of the personal favourites of the girl, boy and little fecker.

BASE RULES

1. BOYS ONLY
2. NO GIRLS
3. TOP SECERT
4. CLUB MEMBERS ONLY

NO GIRLS

THE IMPORTANCE OF HAVING A GOOD BASE OR HUT. A LOT OF OUR GAMES REVOLVED AROUND OUR GANG HQ. IT WAS SUCH A GREAT MULTI-PURPOSE SPACE.

IN ONE CORNER WE WOULD STASH THE DAILY PAGE 3 CUTOUTS THAT WE BOUGHT ON ROTATION, BUT THE REAL FUN HAPPENED THE ONE NIGHT OF THE WEEK WHEN WE ALLOWED GIRLS IN.

EENY MEENY MINY MOE

Most of the games for the boys and girls around our way started by doing a dip:
'Icky ocky horses gocky, icky ocky out.'

'Eeny, meeny, miny, moe,
Catch a ****** by the toe.
If it screams let him go,
Eeny, meeny, miny, moe.'

'My mother and your mother were
    washing clothes,
My mother punched your mother right
    in the nose.
[The colour chosen is spelled out.
Whoever gets the last letter is 'it'.]
What colour was her blood?'

'There is a party on the hill, will you come?
With your own cream currents and your own
    cream bun?
Who is your very best chum in this entire
    whole circle?
Fiona will be there with her ribbons in her hair
    and her knickers inside out.'

TOP TITS

IF FOUR PEOPLE ARE IN THE DIP AND YOU WANT TO BE FIRST OUT, YOU DO THE DIP AND USE 'EENY, MEENY, MINY, MOE' OR 'IP DIP, DOG SHIT'.

PAGE THREE

FACT

43% OF IRISH '80S BOYS USED TO PRETEND TO BE READING THE SUN AT HOME WHEN THEY WERE REALLY LOOKING AT PAGE 3. 98% OF IRISH '80S BOYS' PARENTS KNEW THAT THEIR SONS WERE NOT INTERESTED IN THE NEWS.

SPIN THE BOTTLE

I hated the game Nervous. This involved taking turns feeling the extremities, member of the opposite sex's body before slowly working your hands in towards the more intimate areas. Once you felt uncomfortable, the shout of 'I'm nervous' would go out. The girls and myself (except Alice Keegan) would say 'I'm nervous' once a boy got near our knees or elbows. On the other hand, the boys, no matter what you did, would not say the submission word. Jennifer Whelan had the most disgusting wart-filled hand, yet none of the boys would ever say 'I'm nervous'.

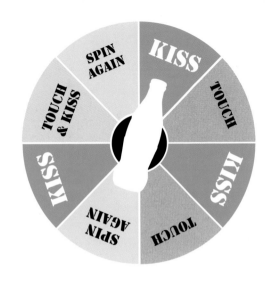

RUN!

Kiss Chase

Image: David J. Gaunt

We all enjoyed Spin the Bottle, Truth or Dare, and Doctors and Nurses, and how only a few of us got glandular fever I will never know. There were a few naughty games, now that I think about it. Kiss Chase was always my nightmare game. I was not the quickest person and I had quite a lot of puppy fat until I was 18, and therefore could not catch any of the fit, good-looking boys. It was kind of weird that when the boys were 'on' – I was always too quick to be caught, even when I slowed to a walk. That blonde bitch Alice Keegan was the quickest, yet she was always caught and ended up shifting 12 boys one afternoon.

We were all wannabe monkeys. Anything that could be climbed was climbed such as trees and anything that had a roof you could sit on. We would sit up there and survey all that was going on in our world.

There were lots of great games like

RELIEVIO
SQUARES
QUEENIE-I-O
RED ROVER
POLIO ♥
BULLDOG CHARGE

– ah the memories!

IF YOU ARE 'ON' FOR BULLDOG –
CALL THE WEAKEST, PUNIEST,
SLOWEST-LOOKING KID FIRST.

A lot of time was spent building swings from a piece of rope tied to a tree and a tyre. If we could not get our hands on a tyre (which was rare), we would tie a big knot on the end of the rope for the seat but that used to wreck the goolies! Around my estate we would make a swing from a lamppost, and within a week the council would come out and take it down. We would then put it back up, and then they would take it down again in what became a drawn-out ongoing battle. Then the clever feckers put a black grease substance all over the pole, so we could not do it anymore. They won that battle but as I lived in one of their houses – let me assure you that I have won the war.

Football was the main game and we would be out on 3/5 and You're In, World Cup, Heads and Volleys and massive 23-a-side matches. The shouts of 'last man back', 'bagsy', 'next goal winner', 'no aces' and 'fly goalies' would be made and the most important thing in the world was winning that match. If it was early or late, and you were left on your own, solos/keepie uppies would entertain you for a good hour.

73% OF IRISH '80'S KIDS CLAIM TO HAVE GOT OVER 100 SOLOS/ KEEPIE UPPIES.

A GUIDE TO
1980s
FOOTBALL

FLY GOALIES

BAGSY BE PAUL McGRATH

ONE GOALIE!

TWO TEAMS

1.THE CONCEPT:
When you and your friends want to play a game of football and there is an odd number of you – then this is the game for you!

2.THE RULES:
Teams are divided equally – players with more skill should be paired with less skillful friends. The odd person out, or unfortunate one, is then put into goals. Teams then compete against each other. Players on each team compete against other teams. You can name your team after your favourite football team or name it after an international team of your choosing. This then changes the game of 'One Goalie – Two Teams' into the similar game of 'World Cup – One Goalie, Two Teams'.

3.THE GOAL:
Try to keep score as fairly as possible – some players are not so good at this. The game ends when either the goalie is too tired or bored to continue, a player or players get called in for their dinner or if the sun goes down and bedtime is then called. This game can then be continued tomorrow and for each day until the end of summer.

BAGS NOT IN!

I loved trying to smash the street light with a football and then to get hold of a spanner to undo the 'DANGER' panel at the bottom of the lamppost to reveal the switch and all the wires - they really were electrifying times!

Image: brownus – Andrew

DANGER

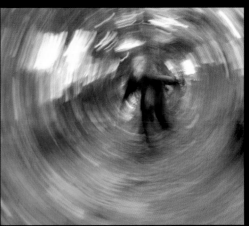

Image: Catherine – daisycottagedonegal

8% OF IRISH 80'S KIDS SAID THEY WERE ELECTROCUTED WHEN THEY WERE YOUNG. MOST OCCURRED FROM COMING INTO CONTACT WITH ELECTRIC FENCES, WHILE JOHN PAUL COUNTED HIS ELECTRIC SHOCK THERAPY.

While the boys were busy playing stupid football, we were busy spinning around, getting dizzy and falling down, then lying on our backs gazing at clouds trying to make shapes out of them. ♥

BLIND MAN'S BLUFF

Blind Man's Bluff with Granny's aul' smelly scarf in the hallways of her house on a Sunday evening with all the cousins.

SMASHING MARBLES UNDER A STEEL SHORE WAS A REGULAR PASTIME FOR ME.

KERBIES

Kerbs (kurbs or kerbies) was a great game around the estates. I have recently been informed that a heck of a lot of 'proper culchies' (the ones that live on farms and one-off houses) have never heard of kerbs. I suppose I will give an explanation for the country folk in case they try to play it on their regional roads and cause our ditches to become clogged up with balls.

One person would stand on the roadside kerb of a housing estate, with the opposing player on the opposite kerb. One player would throw a ball at the opposing player's kerb. If the ball hit the kerb and returned over half way back across the road, that player then had an opportunity to stand in the middle of the road to hit the kerb at a shorter distance. If a miss then occurred, the player who was standing on the kerb could grab the ball and throw it at the player who was trying to run from the middle of the road back to his/her kerb. If the player was hit before returning to their kerb, the other player then had their chance in the middle.

IN A RECENT LATE-NIGHT KERBS COMPETITION AT A SECRET LOCATION AT 5AM AFTER COPPER FACE JACKS, FOUR '80S BOYS TOOK ON FOUR '80S GIRLS. THE SCORE FINISHED 3-1 TO THE GIRLS, WHICH PROVES THAT GIRLS ARE BETTER THAN BOYS AT ONE GAME.

TEN POINTS FOR OVER A MOVING CAR

NIKNAKS

niknaks (nick nocks) was the game of choice most evenings. we would torment half the houses around our way by knocking on the doors or ringing the bells before running away. old man sonny was some oul' fecker. he would regularly come running out of his house in his long johns with saggy moobs on show after a niknak. he was surprisingly quick for an eighty year old and he would come wielding an iron poker, so we had to be fast. we developed a hybrid version of niknaks around Halloween each year, for the other people in the area who had 'crossed' us during the year. this version involved ringing the bell just after we had thrown a blackcat banger in the letterbox.

TOP TIPS

WANT TO IMPRESS THE GANG? HERE IS HOW TO MAKE MICE FLY... WHEN COLLECTING FOR THE BONFIRE COMMENCES, GET YOUR HANDS ON AN OUL' ROLLED UP CARPET AND PLACE IT IN A DITCH FOR STORAGE, PREFERABLY BESIDE THE FIELD WHERE THE BONFIRE WILL BE. WHEN YOU TAKE THE CARPET OUT OF THE DITCH ON OCTOBER 30TH, IT SHOULD BE NICE AND DAMP AND FULL OF MICE. AS THE CARPET IS MOVED, MICE WILL BEGIN TO FLEE. STAMP ON THE MICE TO KILL A FEW. PICK THEM UP BY THE TAIL ON THE QT AND HEAD TOWARDS THE BONFIRE TO A GROUP OF YOUNGER KIDS. PRETEND TO TIE YOUR LACE BESIDE THE KIDS WITH YOUR BACK TO THEM. LIGHT A BLACKCAT AND PLACE IT UNDER A MOUSE AND WALK AWAY. BANG — YOU HAVE A FLYING MOUSE, WITH KIDS SQUEALING AND RUNNING FOR COVER.

Black Cat BANGER

10
CHINA

I COULD REALLY TALK ABOUT MY FAVOURITE TIME OF THE YEAR ALL DAY — HALLOWEEN. THE MORNING AFTER THE BONFIRE, WE WOULD SPEND TIME GOING AROUND PICKING UP ALL THE USED FIREWORKS, BEFORE EMPTYING THE LITTLE BITS OF UNUSED 'GUNPOWDER' ONTO A SHEET OF PAPER. WE WOULD THEN SET FIRE TO THE SHEET OF PAPER AND GET READY FOR THE HUGE ANTI-CLIMAX THAT HAPPENED ONCE THE GUNPOWDER WENT OFF. IT VERY, VERY, VERY VAGUELY LOOKED LIKE THE GENIE SWIRL FROM WHEN THE LAMP WAS RUBBED IN ALADDIN. GOOD TIMES WERE ALSO HAD WHEN WE WOULD BREAK THE STICK OFF A SCREAMER OR ROCKET BEFORE SETTING IT ALIGHT AND SENDING IT DOWN THE ROAD, BOUNCING OFF KERBS TRYING TO HIT SOMEONE.

ORIGAMI
FORTUNE TELLER

1

PHOTOCOPY THE TEMPLATE.

2

FOLD UP ALL CORNERS SO THAT ALL THE POINTS MEET IN THE MIDDLE.

3

IT SHOULD NOW LOOK LIKE THIS. FLIP IT OVER.

4

FOLD UP ALL CORNERS SO THAT ALL THE POINTS MEET IN THE MIDDLE.

5

IT SHOULD NOW LOOK LIKE THIS.

6

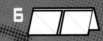

NOW FOLD THE TOP BACK.

7

WORK YOUR FINGERS INTO THE FOUR CORNERS FROM THE FOLD SIDE – WORK THE CREASES TO FORM THE FOUR POINTS.

WHAT WILL YOUR FUTURE HOLD?

PHOTOCOPY AND FILL IN YOUR OWN ANSWERS

Image: Becky Farley

KNOW YOUR FUTURE

The origami fortune-teller game was great fun. Sometimes we would right dares inside when we wanted to kiss certain boys, but most of the time we would have love, life and happiness predictions!

KICK THE CAN

Image: Joanna Hollingworth

FACT

98% OF '80S IRISH KIDS DID NOT USE A CAN WHEN PLAYING TIP/KICK THE CAN. A LAMPPOST WAS THE USUAL CHOICE.

Most evenings around my way, we would have a big game of Tip/Kick the Can before retiring to our base to try to entice young wans in for more shifting.

BAN HAPPY CLAPPING

Happy clapping, tennis balls juggled against the wall and skipping were all played for hours on end – so simple yet so much fun!

DIN DINS

eep
eep

DOLPHIN HUNT

During the days when we were all 'footballed out', Manhunt was played. It really was a great game, except when you would be searching for some fecker for ages, only to realise he had gone in for his dinner and to watch Home and Away.

CHINESE BURNS

FACT

chinese burns was a great 'game'. I gave out a fair share of 3rd degree ones in my time.

THIS 'GAME' IS ONLY KNOWN AS A CHINESE BURN IN IRELAND, ENGLAND, AUSTRALIA AND NEW ZEALAND. OTHER NAMES FOR IT AROUND THE GLOBE INCLUDE: INDIAN BURN, INDIAN RUB, INDIAN RUG BURN, BUFFALO SKIN, SNAKE BITE, POLICEMAN'S GLOVE, HUNDRED NEEDLES, BARBED WIRE, NEEDLES AND FRENCH CUFF.

we used to mill a big rock off the tarmac on the road before quickly getting down to sniff the dent in the rock. the dent smells exactly like a guinness fart. I have not got a clue who discovered this but it's a FACT.

FART

Not sure if these are games but we all used to really enjoy throwing rocks and stones into water. It really didn't matter if it was a river, a pond, the sea or a puddle – once you got a splash. Also, rolling sideways down any hill, or riding anything with wheels down a hill, or racing on anything with wheels in general, was great fun.

Image: Andrew Doak

LBL
LOUD BUT LOVELY

I remember playing

CONKERS

WHACK

TOP TIPS

STORE CONKERS UP THE CHIMNEY OR IN THE
HOT-PRESS FOR THE FOLLOWING YEAR. AFTER
A YEAR YOU TAKE THEM OUT AND THEY ARE
LIKE GOLFBALLS. ONE OF MY CONKERS WON
24 CONSECUTIVE MATCHES IN '89.

The Ouija Board was a game (or was it?) we all played when I had a few girls over for a 'hop' in my house. It was very scary and one time, just after my puppy's father (Kojak) had been knocked down and killed, the wagon Aileen spelt out that Kojak said my pup (Fluffy) hated me and that I was a bitch.

R I P ⬭ **C A T**

> **78% OF '80S IRISH KIDS WHO MESSED WITH A OUIJA BOARD BELIEVED THAT THERE WAS REAL SUPERNATURAL STUFF GOING ON AT THE TIME.**

Bash the Letter/Bash 'em IRA/catch and Bash was probably my favourite game. This involved two 3/4/5/6/7-a-side teams. One team would be 'on' while the other team huddled together to choose a word so that each member of the team had one letter each. So if five were on a team, a chosen word might be 'shite'. The team that was 'on' would then chase down each of the opposing team in the hope of beating and torturing the letters (S,H,I,T,E) out of them in order to guess the word selected. No holds were barred and my personal favourite technique that never failed to extract the letter was to take the person's runner off, while my team took turns to wee in it. Four of my team would then force the detainee's mouth open by pinching and eye-gouging, while I poured the wee from the runner into the mouth.

CHiPS

Role play (not the sexy kind) was massive. We would play cops and robbers with our guns in holsters, batons and plastic handcuffs. We would cycle around on our BMXs pretending to be CHiPs after stealing the mother and father's shades thinking we were the bee's knees. Playing army used to cause ructions around our way. Fist-fights would be had when someone got shot by another 'who was supposed to be dead'. Another was playing Ghostbusters and Teenage Mutant Ninja Turtles. Rows would occur again because nobody wanted to be Winston. Then when playing Turtles, everyone wanted to be Leonardo because he had the cool swords and had the most chance of getting into April O'Neill's pants.

21%

MICHELANGELO

RAPHAEL **6%**

THE SURVEY RESULTS OF 100 '80S IRISH KIDS WHEN ASKED WHO THEIR PREFERRED TEENAGE MUTANT NINJA TURTLE WAS:

DONATELLO

5%

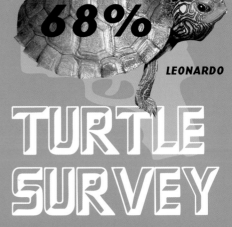

68%

LEONARDO

TURTLE SURVEY

Robbing car signs with a knife from the house .... I had a nice little collection going on my shelf at home. The Merc signs were the most sought after, and you would be surprised at how difficult it is to yank them off.

IF YOU WISH TO STEAL A MERC SIGN, A LITTLE HACKSAW IS WELL WORTH INVESTING IN. OTHERWISE, THE ONLY WAY TO DO IT IS TO STAND ON THE BONNET AND KICK IT OFF.

Image: Kevin A.K.

I LOVED HUNTING FOR
CATS WITH MY GAT. I
HAD A BLACK WIDOW WITH
A FOREARM SUPPORT.
I COULD KILL A CAT
FROM 50 FEET. CROUCH
TO ONE KNEE, SQUINT
THE LEFT EYE, STICK
OUT THE TONGUE,
DRAW THE ELASTIC
BACK, TAKE AIM ...
MEEEEEEEEEEEEEEOW...

HOPSCOTCH
SUCKS

I loved rounders as long as it was played with
a tennis racquet. I was great at the one-arm
catches to get the whole team out. While I am
here, can I just say that hopscotch was crap. All
the girls around my way played this at home and
in school. What is the point of it? One leg, two
legs, one leg.

**Feeling knackered at the
end of every day from playing.**

CHAPTER 3

THE SCHOOL

Ah the memories! Putting on your manky uniform; listening to the snap, crackle and pop of your breakfast as you shat yourself thinking about how you should have finished your Maths homework the night before instead of playing that last game of Tip the Can; packing up your jam sandwiches, and trudging your way towards school. The '80s were an interesting time in our educational history. There was a big shift from the old-school alcoholic priests and specialists of torture (a.k.a. nuns) to normal Joe-soap teachers. Corporal punishment was banned in 1982, we were told, but a few of the oul' boys and women found it hard to change their spots. You would still get the odd hard-finger prod between the shoulder blades for playing football on the grass at lunch or for stamping on the free milk cartons which you aimed at the Junior Infants as they ran past. But while we may have got the odd slap, most '80s kids are fortunate to have mainly good memories of their school days.

Image: Seán Dreilinger

MASH-E-DE-HUL-E?

21% OF '80S KIDS WERE SLAPPED/ SMACKED/WHIPPED BY A TEACHER IN SCHOOL.

The fear of the first day in primary school, as the parents would try to reassure you and tell you about all the new friends you would make, but you knew and were incredibly scared of a few of the older ones who hung around your area… the rumours of heads being flushed down toilets and kids being hung from windows were to the front of the mind as you took those tentative steps from your house that first morning. The one thing that you had going for you was that you knew you had the coolest schoolbag going – 'Teenage Mutant Hero Turtles'. I met a few of the older ones at various houses along the way that first walk to primary school – I don't remember the parents ever coming along on the first morning.

TOP DOG

I would not say I was scared
starting secondary school, as
I knew I would be able to batter
most lads up to 3rd year. It
was a bit of a pain in the arse
though, going from being top dog,
one of the eldest and the main
man in the school in 6th class
to beginning on the bottom rung
of the ladder in first year
as the youngest again. ☠

43% OF '80S KIDS WERE
VERY SCARED OF STARTING
SECONDARY SCHOOL.

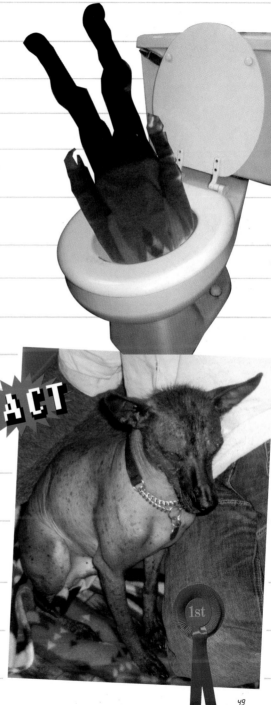

Image: David Denny

FACT

I used to love that hour or two
in Junior Infants and Senior
Infants when you were allowed
to play with toys and have a nap.

49

IN ENGLAND
THE GREEN CROSS CODE MAN WAS
A COSTUMED SUPERHERO
CHARACTER CREATED TO TEACH
YOUNG CHILDREN THE CODE.

IN THE ADS HE WAS PLAYED
BY DAVID PROWSE, WHO
WAS DARTH VADER
IN STAR WARS.

STOP
PLEASE

THE SAFE CROSS CODE

remember,
one, look for a safe place
two, don't hurry, stop
and wait,
three, look all around
and listen
before you cross the road,

remember,
four, let all the traffic
pass you five,
then walking
straight across you
six, keep watching,
that's the safe cross
code!!!!!

CHILDREN CROSSING
WITH ODD HEADS

I remember everyone walking or cycling to school. You and your parents knew you would be grand after watching The Safe Cross Code. Anyone remember the brilliant Safe Cross Code colouring book to go with it? Parents driving you to school was pretty much unheard of back then. ♥

SCHOOL SAMBO *Popularity*

PLAIN OL'
CHEESE
14%

THE CLASSIC
HAM &CHEESE
16%

CORNED BEEF
From a Tin - Get in!
23%

The Staple Diet
JAM
28%

19%

OTHERS
Salad – Too wet to eat by lunchtime
Tinned Salmon – Pink Squidgee
Egg Mayonnaise – The Risktaker
Boiled Egg – The Repercussion
Butter/Margarine – The Unoriginal

* Note
All sambos are made with white bread only. This was a time when only white bread existed and brown bread was seen as a healthy luxury/excess.

'THE MA MAKING ME JAM SANDBOS/SAMBOS EVERYDAY FOR 14 BLEEDIN YEARS.'

NATURE TABLE

We used to collect a heap of stuff from our gardens and parks for the Nature Table in school. One year I got Mammy to buy a pumpkin and claimed my Dad grows them in the back garden for the Autumn table.

I remember being absolutely freezing in school once October and November hit. Sitting in ice-cold prefab classrooms, frosted breath leaving the mouth and that one fecker of a teacher that would not let you keep your coats on even though he kept his on! There was no such a thing as a day off back then because the heating was not working … otherwise we would have been off from October to March!

ICE ICE BABY

TOP TIPS

MURDER, SHE WROTE

IF YOU HAD A HEAP OF HOMEWORK DUE THE NEXT DAY, IF THERE WAS A DOUBLE EPISODE OF MURDER SHE WROTE ON AFTER SUPERMARKET SWEEP AT 10AM, OR IF YOU JUST DIDN'T FANCY GOING TO SCHOOL – ALL YOU HAD TO DO WAS TO PUT YOUR FOREHEAD ON THE RADIATOR FOR AT LEAST 10 MINUTES. THIS MADE YOUR EYES SWELL AND YOUR 'TEMPETURE' RISE SO WHEN THE MAMMY WOULD PUT HER HAND ON YOUR FOREHEAD SHE WOULD GET A FRIGHT AND TELL YOU THOSE AMAZING WORDS, 'THERE WILL BE NO SCHOOL FOR YOU TOMORROW.' IF YOU PUT ON A REALLY GOOD SHOW, A SPOONFUL OF THE PURPLE CALPOL MAY HAVE EVEN BEEN ORDERED (SEE THE GOODIES CHAPTER)!!

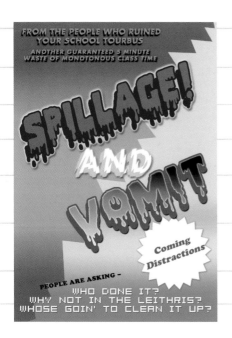

FROM THE PEOPLE WHO RUINED
YOUR SCHOOL TOURBUS
ANOTHER GUARANTEED 5 MINUTE
WASTE OF MONOTONOUS CLASS TIME

SPILLAGE!
AND
VOMIT

Coming Distractions

PEOPLE ARE ASKING –
WHO DONE IT?
WHY NOT IN THE LEITHRIS?
WHOSE GOIN' TO CLEAN IT UP?

Be a Good Girl Now and Clean That Up

Any time anything was spilt in a classroom – a girl would be asked to clean it up!

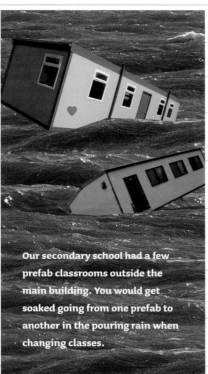

Our secondary school had a few prefab classrooms outside the main building. You would get soaked going from one prefab to another in the pouring rain when changing classes.

SEXISM

Lots of sexism actually! We girls had to cook the after-match and training tea and serve it to the boys on the hurling, football, soccer, quiz and the master-debating teams. After every match, the girls had to wash up the boys' teacups and plates, while hoping that they left a few Fig Rolls or Mikado (they never left any biscuits).

'Careers Counselling' was also a bit of a joke. Some aul' fella telling us girls that we could be a nun or a teacher, nurse or civil servant and that it didn't really matter anyway as we only had to work for a few years until we found a man to marry us.

TIRED OF BEING THE BUTT OF THE JOKE?

FACT

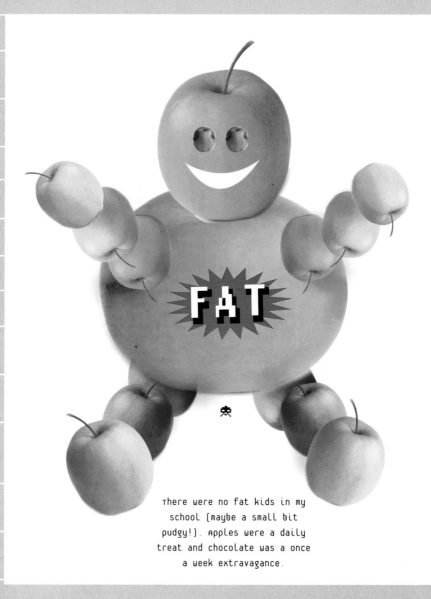

FAT

There were no fat kids in my school (maybe a small bit pudgy!). Apples were a daily treat and chocolate was a once a week extravagance.

The tragic loss of free strawberry milk
and the campaign to get it back!

MILK ME

THE DAIRY COMPANY WHO PRODUCED SCHOOL STRAWBERRY MILK WAS INUNDATED WITH REQUESTS TO REINTRODUCE THE PRODUCT (SOME CONTAINING THREATS BY 9 YEAR OLDS THAT THEY WOULD BOYCOTT THEIR PRODUCTS FOR THE REST OF THEIR LIVES).

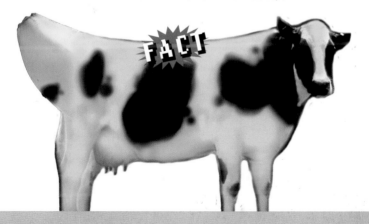

FACT

DÚN AN DORAS

♥ The dentist coming around once a year
and giving out pink and yellow tablets

**27% OF '80S KIDS REMEMBER
TAKING TABLETS GIVEN TO THEM
BY A DENTIST IN THEIR SCHOOL**

The only way you could 'stand out' in school with the uniform was to have the best shoes. If you did not have a pair of Doc Martens or Kickers in September you were considered waaaaaaaay down the food chain. The only other chance you had to show off was during PE. No matter how shite at football you were, you would wear the latest jersey and a quality pair of football boots. The girls could not really tell who the better players were in the year. So as long as you looked the part, you would go up in their estimations.

FACT

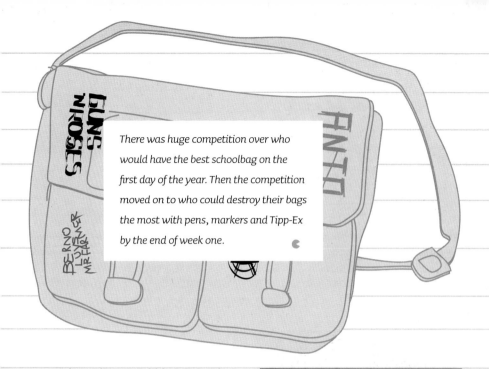

There was huge competition over who would have the best schoolbag on the first day of the year. Then the competition moved on to who could destroy their bags the most with pens, markers and Tipp-Ex by the end of week one.

I used to love nailing people with rubber bands and jockin' people in the yard. Thumb tacks on chairs and putting a heavy book on the top of a half-open door to hit fellow classmates and/or a teacher was also good craic.

TOP TIPS

WHEN SOMEONE YOU DON'T LIKE AND WANT TO EMBARRASS IS WEARING TROUSERS WITH A BELT, SMUGGLE A PEN KNIFE OR SCISSORS OUT TO THE SCHOOL YARD. AS YOU AND AN ACCOMPLICE SNEAK UP TO AN UNSUSPECTING JOCKIN' TARGET, SLIP THE KNIFE OR SCISSORS UNDER THE BELT AT THE BACK AND SNIP. AS THE 'SNIP' OF THE BELT OCCURS – YOUR BUDDY YANKS THE TROUSERS DOWN.

FROM OUTSIDE THE CLASSROOM...
A DISTRACTION LIKE NO OTHER...

EVERYBODY REMEMBERS

VIEWERS ARE ASKING THE QUESTIONS
WHO WILL SUMMON HIM IN?
CAN WE KEEP HIM?
AND SIMPLY - WHY?

THE DAY THE DOG CAME INTO CLASS

A GUARANTEED 8 MINUTES OF EUPHORIA

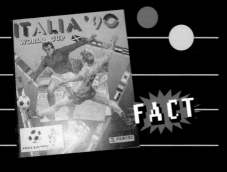

Image: coderkind

FACT

The gushy or grushy - usually involved someone throwing un-needed Panini/Merlin football stickers or POGS or even sweets on the ground in front of a gang of excited younger lads/lassies in the schoolyard to fight over.... great entertainment!

61% OF '80S KIDS SURVEYED BELIEVE THE WORD IS PRONOUNCED GUSHY, COMPARED TO 39% WHO BELIEVE IT IS PRONOUNCED GRUSHY.

GRUSHY

Having a smoke upstairs on the bus on the way to school, just to be a mad lad.

RIGHT SAID FRED

Does anybody else remember Fred (he was gigantically tall), who came to national schools as a one-man circus? His brother also toured with their family troupe, Corvenio's. I have crystal-clear memories of how exciting it was when they came to town. Fred could eat fire, juggle swords, unicycle and make your teachers look stupid. What more could a national school full of kids want?

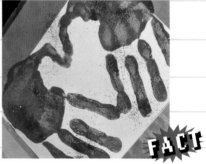

The 'importance' of Valentine cards. Once Christmas holidays were well and truly over, that month before February 14th would be full of planning and nervous apprehension. You would get Mammy to bring you to the shop to buy glitter and markers to make the Valentine cards for the boys in your class that you fancied. You and the girls would sit around and plan who would give cards to the three hotties – Michael, Anthony and Derek. If a boy gave you a card it would be the best day of your little life – even if it usually consisted of a white A4 page folded in half with 'To Anne, from Derek' written in pencil.

44% OF MALE '80S KIDS SURVEYED RECEIVED A HOMEMADE VALENTINE'S CARD FROM A CLASSMATE IN SCHOOL.

2

1

3

The walk of shame when you threw something at the bin and missed.

My school was very poor. We were going through the Michael 'Air' Jordan years and we all loved trying to play basketball. The problem was that we had no basketball or basketball hoops in the yard. So each of us would have to take turns standing like a statue on a chair at either end of the yard with our arms outstretched in a loop. Some of the older lads were very mean and they would regularly 'dunk' you with a football.

MY FIRST BOOK	The fox hunts at night.	The End	Well done

FACT

78% OF '80S KIDS WHO USED SRA IN SCHOOL CHEATED THEIR WAY THROUGH A FEW COLOURS.

Not every school was lucky enough to have SRA. I used to think it was like Karate – moving up a colour every 2nd afternoon (by cheating as there was always an answer sheet floating around in the end of the box).

AN BHFUIL CEAD AGAM DUL GO DTÍ AN LEITHRIS?

Giving the lads a 'banter loaf' in the morning as a way of greeting each other. A banter loaf like, not an aggressive head butt, however the aim was to leave a nice little red mark in the middle of your mate's forehead for the rest of the day.

BATTER BURGER

A bag of chips and a batter burger on the way home from school on a Friday was a real treat.

HALF DAY
FOR BIG SAM

I used to love getting a half day or no homework when your county won the All-Ireland and the team came to visit. Thank God I was not from Dublin or some other crap county like that!

CHAPTER 4

THE GOODIES

Sweets tasted better in the '80s, FACT. Yes they were loaded with e numbers, yes they were responsible for rotting the teeth out of our heads which left us with some pretty gruesome-looking communion photos, but they were so damn satisfying. Back when Snickers were Marathons and Starbursts were Opal Fruits, sweets ran the gamut from the gimmicky (Edible Paper), to the tasteless in every sense of the word (Candy Watches) and just plain disgusting (Pink Chocolate). So dig in and enjoy a banquet of Burger Bites, Wham Bars, Wibbly Wobbly Wonders, all washed down with some Caaaaaaaaavan Cola.

PENNY SWEETS

HAIL TO THE POWER

THE BOTTLE HAS SPOKEN

THIS WAS MY FAVOURITE 'SWEET'. THERE WERE MANY, MANY, MANY NIGHTS THAT THE FOREHEAD WOULD BE PLACED ON A RADIATOR OR UNDER THE HOT TAP FOR A FEW MINUTES BEFORE THE TREK TO MAMMY.

Barry: 'Oh Mam, I have a headache and one minute I am hot and the next I am cold.'

Mammy: 'Barry, here have some Calpol. I got the new 6+ one now that you are seven.'

Barry: 'No thanks Mam, I am feeling a lot better already.'

The pink Calpol with the purple label was absolutely gorgeous, but the orange-flavoured 6+ one was rotten.

ACID DROPS

Acid drops were the sourest of sour hard sweets. They were ball-shaped, bright yellow in colour and came in yellow plastic wrappers. I hated them but I would regularly buy them to go around the estate and give them to little kids. I took great pleasure in watching five and six year olds' faces turn inside out and cry with pain from the drops.

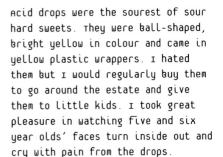

TERMINATE JELLY BABIES

FLYING SAUCERS WERE ONE OF MY FAVOURITE
SWEETS GROWING UP. THEY WERE TWO MULTICOLOURED
DISCS OF RICE PAPER WITH A FIZZY POWDER INSIDE.
THERE WERE FOUR WAYS OF EATING THEM:

- BITE A LITTLE HOLE ON ONE SIDE AND SHAKE THE FIZZ INTO YOUR GOB.

- PUT IT ON YOUR TONGUE AND WAIT FOR IT TO DISSOLVE, LIKE SKIPS
  CRISPS, TO GET TO THE FIZZ.

- TAKE A BIG BITE OR SHOVE IT IN WHOLE AND CHEW.

- BREAK IT APART AND SNORT THE FIZZ OFF A TABLE.

QUARTER DROP OF...

I used to love going in to the sweet shops
to get a quarter of my favourite sweets. The
pick and mix in supermarkets and cinemas
have really taken over now, but it is not the
same as getting the old woman in the local
shop to reach up and take down the big glass
jars full of Cough Drops, Apple Drops,
Satin Sweets, Liquorice Allsorts, Jelly Bears,
Jelly Eggs, Snooker Balls Chewing Gum,
Pineapple Chunks, Cola Cubes and Cola
Bottles – Fizzy or Plain.

STRAW-
BERRY
BON
BONS

NO.
LEMON
BON
BONS

SUGAR
ME

CHOCOLATE

Jeez, I used to dream about these. These were similar to normal Lion Bars except there was heaps of peanut butter in the middle where the wafer usually is.

BRING BACK PEANUT BUTTER LION BARS!

FACT

Klipso Bar: I was a big fan of these. They used to wreck my teeth, but hey – so does smoking. Rock-hard toffee on the inside made a perfect weapon at football matches to nail someone taking a throw-in or a corner. God help the linesman if he made a wrong offside call.

FREDDO FROG CHOCOLATE BARS WERE MEANT TO BE CHOCOLATE MICE UNTIL A LAST-MINUTE CHANGE OF HEART BY CADBURY.

BAR CHART

Cadbury Freddo Frog and Taz Bars – The one problem I had with the Freddo Frog bar was its size. It was barely a mouthful for 8-year-old Barry. The caramel-filled version of a Freddo was the Taz Bar, which was named after the Tasmanian Devil Looney Toons character. This was much nicer than a Cadbury's Caramel!

GOOD

AVERAGE

BAD

CABANA BAR | CARAMAC BAR | FREDDO FROG | MACAROON BARS | TAZ BARS | STARBAR (NIBBLED ON) | KLIPSO BAR

WELCOME TO

Drawda

HOME OF THE STAH BAH

Star Bars are as famous in Ireland for slagging off the county Louth accent as they are for the nice taste. Just go to Drogheda or Bettystown or Laytown and say 'Do you like staaaaaaaaar Baaaaars?' to anyone and you should get a slap. The original ad for the bar was a really weird one. It featured a girl walking a horse which was dragging a barge along a canal – your guess is as good as mine.

FACT

THE STAR BAR HAS BEEN RELAUNCHED UNDER A FEW DIFFERENT GUISES – MORO PEANUT IN IRELAND, NUNCH, NUDGE, PEANUT BOOST, AND IN GERMANY IT IS CALLED WUNDERBAR. THIS BAR WAS ALSO CADBURY'S FIRST REAL ATTEMPT TO TAKE ON THE JUGGERNAUTS THAT ARE MARS AND MARATHON BARS IN THE '70S AND '80S.

OAP DELIGHT

FACT

FRY'S TURKISH DELIGHT

THIS DELICIOUS BAR IS STILL ON SALE AND CONTAINS A HELL OF A LOT FEWER CALORIES THAN MOST OTHER CHOCOLATE BARS. SO LADIES, WHEN A MAN LEAVES YOU, REACH FOR THE TURKISH DELIGHTS AND NOT THE CARAMEL, MARS, GOLDEN CRISPS, WHOLENUTS, BOURNEVILLE, ETC...

SECRET BAR ♥

The Secret Bar was pretty special. It was similar enough to a Walnut Whip in that it had a creamy mousse centre. The bar was probably as famous for its TV ad as it was for its beautiful taste. It featured a very pretty lady in a train carriage who is then asked to guard 'the Secret Bar' with her life by a very handsome man. Two hoodlums then chase the handsome fella away, obviously looking for the Secret Bar. As soon as handsome man disappears, the pretty lady cannot help but wolf down the Secret Bar, albeit rather seductively. Handsome man returns to get his bar and the pretty lady drags him onto the seat and shifts the head off him, as the line 'you can't trust anyone to keep a secret' is said by a man with a deep voice.

THE CONFECTIONERY PREVIOUSLY KNOWN AS		NEW NAME
MARATHON	→	SNICKERS
OPAL FRUITS	→	STARBURST
GALAXY COUNTERS	→	MINSTRELS

Minstrels

SMILEY BARS

These were my favourite bar growing up. They were chocolate on the outside with an orangey toffee in the middle. When you pulled it apart the chocolate would crack off and you could get straight to the orange toffee.

versas

vice

TOUCHDOWN

I loved Touchdown Bars. They were a finger wafer bar consisting of four layers with chocolate cream between, completely covered in chocolate. They came in purple and red wrapping for 10p and Time Outs are not a patch on them!

CHEWY-ROT-YOUR-TEETH BARS & SWEETS

POSTMAN PAT SWEETS, REFRESHER BARS/SWEETS, SKITTLES, WHOPPA SPEARMINT AND COLA BARS

THE ORIGINAL OPAL FRUIT SWEETS ONLY CAME IN FOUR FLAVOURS – ORANGE, STRAWBERRY, LEMON AND LIME. I ALWAYS THOUGHT THERE WERE OTHERS...

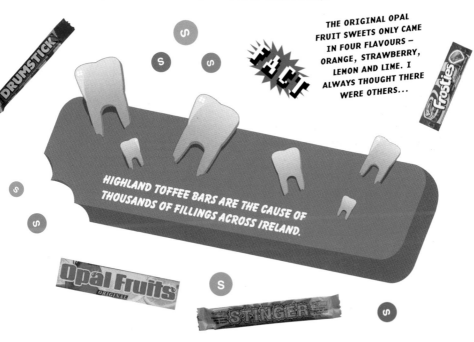

HIGHLAND TOFFEE BARS ARE THE CAUSE OF THOUSANDS OF FILLINGS ACROSS IRELAND.

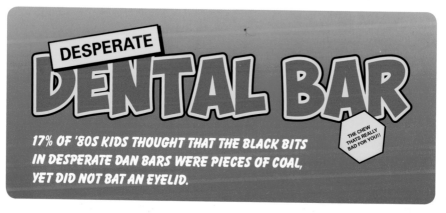

DESPERATE DENTAL BAR

THE CHEW THATS REALLY BAD FOR YOU!!

17% OF '80S KIDS THOUGHT THAT THE BLACK BITS IN DESPERATE DAN BARS WERE PIECES OF COAL, YET DID NOT BAT AN EYELID.

Boy of the No Teeth

ROY OF THE ROVERS BAR WAS A VERY SOUR ONE. IT WAS PINEAPPLE FLAVOUR WITH TINY SOUR BITS THROUGH IT AND A PICTURE OF THE ROY HIMSELF ON THE WRAPPER IN FRONT OF A GOAL IN A STADIUM.

WHERE HAVE YOUR TEETH GONE?

WHAM BAR

Pink, sticky, chewy bar with green and yellow pieces, I think. A few sour bits too, but all I remember is it being very sticky!

FRUIT SALADS

VS

BLACK JACKS

FACT

Black jacks were great as they were another half-decent weapon. Many's a day I spent walking down the street behind a good-looking woman in her lovely new white coat. A little half spit through my teeth was all it took.

BLACK JACKS WERE THE HARDEST SWEETS TO GET AWAY WITH EATING FROM YOUR SECRET STASH WHEN YOUR PARENTS REFUSED YOU A BISCUIT IN THAT HOUR BEFORE YOUR DINNER. YOU JUST COULD NOT HIDE THAT BLACK TONGUE!

PK CHEWING GUMS

JUICY FRUITS

WHO STUCK THE GUM UNDER THE TABLE?

GOLF BALL CHEWING GUMS

HUBBA BUBBA

CHOCOLATE + CHEWING GUM
FAILURE

I USED TO LIKE HUBBA BUBBA BUBBLE GUM MORE THAN MOST CHEWING GUMS, BUT ONCE I TASTED THE CHOCOLATE FLAVOUR ONE IT PUT ME OFF CHEWING GUM FOR THE REST OF MY LIFE. IT WAS ABSOLUTELY RANK.

ICE POPS

DILUTED ORANGE ICE POPS

THE POORMAN'S MR.FREEZE

IF YOU ARE LUCKY ENOUGH TO HAVE DILUTED ORANGE.... BUT TOO POOR FOR A SHOP BOUGHT TREAT –
WHY NOT TRY –

STEP 1:
Fill a reliable and freezer proof mug with a mix of dilute orange and H2O*

STEP 2:
Leave in the freezer overnight/few hours till frozen solid.

STEP 3:
Take out and enjoy!

*as this is a already a scabby treat – don't be stingy with the Miwadi/KiaOra/Etc

we were poor, so Dunnes stores own-brand diluted orange was the only drink in our gaff (except for naggins and naggins of mam's vodka). we had those ice-trays in our little freezer beside all the st bernard fish fingers so we would take the trays out and fill them full of diluted orange. we'd stick them in the freezer for a few hours and we would have ice pops. mam found them one day and threw them into her vodka and thought it was so nice that she went and bought us more ice trays .... that was a great day.

My Granny used to love these. We would be out for the day and she would stop at the shop. Before she came back to the car I knew she would have a Super Split, a Golly Bar and a Bounty Bar. She always let me choose between the Split and the Golly Bar (even though I always went for the Super Split!) and we would then take a finger of Bounty each.

♥

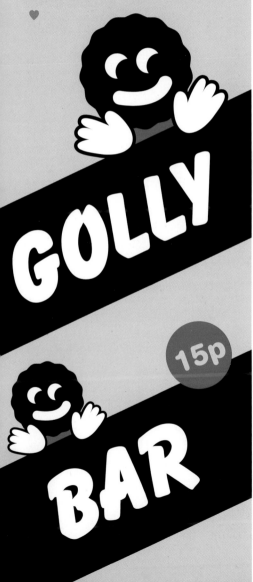

15p

CHILLY WILLY

10p

I used to love floats. Throw a block of ice cream into a glass of anything fizzy and then watch the fizz rise to the top. Get a get 'big' spoon and dip it in to eat the cream fizz.

It just did not seem right watching MacGyver, closing my eyes and imagining him wearing the face off me, without a Fanta Float in my hand on a Saturday. ♥

SCREWBALLS

99S FROM MR WHIPPY WITH EXTRA RASPBERRY BLOOD

SUPER SPLIT

JR ICE POP COUNT

DRACULA'S DEADLY SECRET LOLLIES

A GUIDE TO
FLOATS

Coke floats /
Fanta & Ice Cream /
TK Red Lemonade & Ice Cream

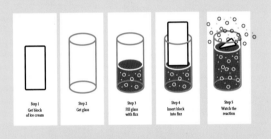

Step 1
Get block of ice cream

Step 2
Get glass

Step 3
Fill glass with fizz

Step 4
Insert block into fizz

Step 5
Watch the reaction

CRISPS

MEANIES

I hate onions and the thought of pickled onions makes me physically sick. Yet I loved pickled onion flavoured Meanies. ♥

CRUNCHO CRISPS
Hot-dog flavoured, rather surprisingly, they tasted nothing like hot dogs!

PIZZA-FLAVOURED TURTLE CRISPS
Rather surprisingly, tasted nothing like pizza – what a shocker!

BURGER BITES

RANCHEROS

SAM SPUDZ

PUB CRISPS

PERRI CRISPS

MA REILLY CRISPS

SKIPS

EDIBLE PAPER

This page is made of edible paper, go on, have a try.

LILT

'The totally tropical taste' was the slogan when LILT was launched in the '70s. It was the drink of choice for me and the lads around the shops in our estate. One visitor to our shop took exception to me slagging him about his LA Gear runners and said the words 'Look at you, drinking a girl's drink (Lilt).'

Remember that game 'Bash 'em IRA' from the Games chapter? — Let me just say that he gave us 26 letters and a few Hail Marys but it didn't stop me. I loved LILT and still do, and I am not ashamed to admit it.

I AM FROM
CAAAAAAAAVAN

FACT

THERE WAS A RUMOUR THAT AN EU BAN CAUSED THE PREMATURE END OF CAVAN COLA DUE TO AN EXCESSIVE AMOUNT OF E NUMBERS AND SUGAR. THIS IS NOT TRUE, CAVAN PEOPLE ARE SO TIGHT THAT THEY DIDN'T WANT TO SPEND MONEY ON PETROL DISTRIBUTING THE COLA TO OTHER COUNTIES.
THIS IS A SECRET, BUT IF YOU WANT SOME CAVAN COLA, HEAD UP TO ANY PUB OR SHOP IN CAVAN AND SAY THIS SECRET PHRASE IN YOUR BEST CAVAN ACCENT AND THEY WILL REACH UNDER THE COUNTER FOR SOME COLA FOR YOU, 'I AM FROM CAAAAAAAVAN, AND I LUUUUVE MONEY.'

CAVAN COLA WAS MY FAVOURITE DRINK, THOUGH: RIDICULOUSLY FIZZY, VERY SWEET, AND SLIGHTLY LIQUORICEY. IT IS PROBABLY BEST KNOWN FOR SENDING KIDS ABSOLUTELY NUTS FROM THE AMOUNT OF SUGARS AND SWEETENERS IT CONTAINED. IN THE LOCAL PUB AS OUR PARENTS GOT LOCKED AND SMOKED THEIR MAJOR EVERY FRIDAY AND SATURDAY, ME AND THE BOYS WOULD BE SWINGING OUT OF THE LIGHTS AND SHITEING ON TOILET PAPER SO WE COULD RUB IT ON THE WALLS, BECAUSE OF CAVAN COLA.

AMERICAN CREAM SODA

The first time I tried it I thought, kill me now, this drink is the nicest drink I have ever tasted and it will never be beaten. I tried it again a few months ago and my teeth still whisper, 'you feckin' ass, don't ever let that pure sugar shite near us again' when I have DTs after a lot of wine with the girls.

♥

Feck your Lucozade and your Club Energizer – drink Football Special. We had a mad teacher from Donegal that coached our school GAA team. Mr Hegarty maintained that this brew from his home county, with its secret mixed fruit, could make a man fight back every wave that rolled in off the Atlantic to strike his fair county's shoreline. He also used to say that any man that drank Football Special would 'never get their comeuppance'.

RED LEMONADE IS ONLY AVAILABLE IN IRELAND

I DRANK TOO MUCH SAYS BOY

EXPATRIATES SAY IT IS ONE OF THE THINGS THEY MISS THE MOST ABOUT BEING HOME.

RED LEMONADE IS NOW ONLY AVAILABLE IN IRELAND DUE TO THE ABUNDANCE OF RED-HAIRED CHILDREN WHO PLAY A VITAL ROLE IN THE CREATION OF THE SOFT DRINK.

RED LEMONADE ONLY EXISTS IN IRELAND BECAUSE THE CHEMICAL USED TO MAKE IT RED IS BANNED ELSEWHERE IN THE WORLD DUE TO THE CARCINOGENS.

STUFF

UNLUCKY BAG OF SHITE

FACT

AMY WINEHOUSE USED TO LOVE SUPERHERO CHEWING GUM AND SAID IN AN INTERVIEW THAT THE FREE TATTOOS INFLUENCED HER TO GET REAL ONES ONCE SHE WAS OLD ENOUGH.

Lucky Bags were a great treat between the birthday and Christmas. Sweets, a colouring book and crayons, a game and a miniature pack of playing cards or a whistle – you didn't know what you would get. It was kind of like the shite stuff you would get from a cheap selection of Christmas crackers.

superhero chewing gum was class. you got free rub-on tattoos that made me look even harder than I was at the age of 6.

GRANDMA WE LOVE YOU
GRANDMA WE DO

I used to stay with my Granny on a Saturday Night. While Granddad and myself were in watching Kenny Live, she would be out in the kitchen making the trifle for after the Sunday Roast.

I would go out during the ad breaks and she would give me chunks of the raw strawberry jelly. ♥

78

THE WONDERS OF
PUSH POPS

PUSH POPS ARE STILL REALLY POPULAR ACROSS THE GLOBE AND DAVID HASSLEHOFF CURRENTLY FRONTS THE SOUTH-EAST ASIA PROMOTIONAL CAMPAIGNS.

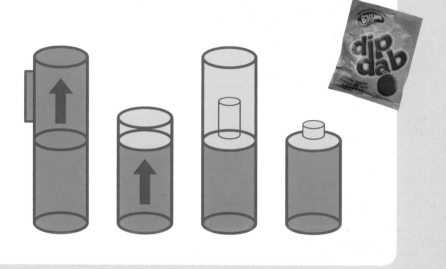

CANDY CIGARETTES
RAINBOW DROPS
SHERBET DIP DABS
SHERBET FOUNTAINS
DOUBLE DIPS
TREBOR DOUBLE AGENTS
DOLLY BEADS
DOLLY WATCHES
2P FLOGS

IF YOU MIX
MENTOS AND COKE
TOGETHER AND FORCE
FEED IT TO A HAMSTER,
IT DOES MAKE THEIR
HEAD EXPLODE.

FACT!

A SOPHISTICATED SODASTREAM

'Get busy with the fizzy.' At the time I thought this was the best invention ever! Fizzy drinks were expensive in the '80s and we only got one 2-litre bottle of Lilt a week. With the Sodastream at home, we now had access to the 'amazing' Cola, Cherryade, and Dandelion and Burdock flavours. The aul' gas canisters of Carbon Dioxide needed to make the fizz were the problem. They ran out after 12 and a half pints of Cola, if I remember correctly. You would then have to trek back to the shop and swap your empty canister for a new one. They were also not the most robust of contraptions. Once you replaced the canisters a few times the seal would loosen and the CO_2 would escape.

LOVE HEARTS ARE A GREAT CURE FOR
HEARTBURN AND BY BUYING THEM FOR
A GIRL ON THE ESTATE IT GUARANTEED
A RAUNCHY HAND-HOLDING ROMP.

CHAPTER 5

THE TOYS

It's amazing that any '80s kid has managed to procreate after the warped ideas of the anatomy given to us by Barbie, Action Man and Operation. I don't think I am being biased when I say that toys in the '80s were far superior to those of any other decade in history! There were fantastic board games, dolls, teddies, action figures, ride-on tractors, toys with lasers, toys for the garden or the beach, and miniature household items to train young girls to become perfect housewives.

There are literally thousands of '80s toys that could be included in this chapter. I have left out a few of the more obvious items like the Rubik's Cube, Transformers, Space Hoppers, Roller Skates and the free toys that we would all get from horsing our way through boxes of cereal. You'll be dying to be a kid again and bask in the glow of the Glo Worm or spend four carefree hours trying to construct Mouse Trap. These 39 toys were the ones that kept me out of trouble when I was a kid.

BOARD GAMES

OPERATION

My early memories of Operation involved worrying about getting sick myself and a 'surgeon' taking out a variety of body parts while I lay naked (with no willy) on a table with my eyes open. We would take turns trying not to touch the sides of the hole from where each body part needed to be delicately extracted. The catchphrase that everyone remembers from the TV ad was 'Here goes his funnybone ...', which meant that whoever had the first go, always went for the funny bone.

THE ADAM'S APPLE WAS THE MOST DIFFICULT BODY PART TO EXTRACT.

FACT

MOUSE TRAP

The idea was to get a mouse around the board, having assembled a brilliantly designed mouse trap. The trap involved a marble, a man flipping into a tub, a falling cage, a boot on a stick, a bath with a hole in it and a zig-zag path. Due to the complicated construction of the trap, there were many malfunctions, which would result in many people's mice escaping capture.

TOP TIPS

FORGET ABOUT PLAYING AND WINNING THE GAME. IT IS A BIG ENOUGH ACHIEVEMENT CONSTRUCTING A WORKING TRAP WITHOUT A STRUCTURAL ENGINEERING DEGREE, SO PUT ALL YOUR TIME AND EFFORT IN TO THAT.

GUESS WHO

Growing up we played our own version of Guess Who. The usual questions about the person's physical appearance such as 'Does your character have red hair?' were banned. Alternatively, we came up with the rule that made your opponent make a judgement call on the person's potential personality, based purely on their looks. So questions like 'Is your person gay?', 'Is your person a Mammy's boy/girl?', or 'Has your person ever murdered someone?', were the norm. Then you had to eliminate the characters on your board. It was pretty surprising how often the opposing player was still able to guess the character correctly.

EARLY VERSIONS OF GUESS WHO FEATURED ONLY 5 WOMEN COMPARED TO 19 MEN ... THE FEMINISTS JUMPED ON THIS ONE TOO, AND IT CHANGED TO 12 WOMEN AND 12 MEN IN THE '90S.

FACT

BATTLESHIP

Battleship was one of my favourite games. I grew up playing a version of it with a pen and paper most evenings with my uncle. Eventually one Christmas I asked Santa for the plastic version of the game, but I hardly played it at all. Give me the pen and paper version any day.

TWISTER

Ah what a game. A few of the women around my way were always up for playing it at free gaffs. Twister was just an excuse to climb all over, rub up against and get yourself into compromising positions with the opposite sex. The hormones would be flying after Twister and it always a gateway game to the likes of spin the bottle or Nervous. 👾

A RECENT STUDY BY UNIVERSITY COLLEGE LEITRIM HAS SHOWN THAT YOUTH PARTICIPATION IN THE GAME OF TWISTER HAS BEEN DIRECTLY LINKED TO 13,477 TEENAGE PREGNANCIES SINCE 1987.

GAELIC GAMES BOARD GAME

Not a lot of people will remember this one. I got the game second hand in the late '80s and the rulebook was missing. It consisted of a green GAA pitch board with goalposts at either end. There were a few plastic players who would move around playing hurling or football as you rolled a dice. I really cannot remember this game too well, if you would like to furnish me with any other details, please email me at barry@gaaistooeasybecause theballisinyourhands.com.

DOLLS/ TEDDIES

CABBAGE PATCH DOLLS

Ugly, with pudgy round faces, stumpy arms and tiny close-together eyes, no not Van Morrison – Cabbage Patch Dolls!! They really were brutal-looking yokes, however they were the most unique dolls going. Each doll came with its own birth date and its own unique name. Once I filled in my details on the paperwork provided as the doll's adoptive parent, I sent it off to the makers. A year later I received my doll's first birthday card in the post!

THEY WERE SO UGLY THAT THEY WERE CUTE.

CUPCAKE DOLLS

Cherry Merry Muffin and Strawberry Shortcake scented dolls. I loved these. Turn their skirts inside out and they transformed into a cupcake with their hats forming the icing. These were our girls' version of Transformers, except much better!

MY LITTLE PONY ♥

Myself and all my friends would ask for a pony every single year without fail on our Santa Claus list. My Little Pony solved my parents'/Santa's problem. I loved My Little Pony's lovely soft brushable mane and tail. I would plait it and try to dye it with bleach and Bovril. There were only six different ponies with different markings, colours and names at the beginning and I had all six, which made all the other girls jealous. The makers then went a bit nuts and released sitting ponies, clothes, baby ponies and pony baths – far too commercial.

TEDDY RUXPIN, THE STORYTELLING BEAR!

The best teddy bear ever? A teddy that told stories more than made up for the mother being in the local every night drinking her pints of Harp. There was a huge shortage of Teddy Ruxpins in the Leinster area one winter in the late '80s, due to hundreds falling off the back of a lorry in Dublin Port.

I had asked for a sharp knife like Crocodile Dundee's and a knuckle duster for my 6th birthday in December, but my mother got offered a cheap Teddy Ruxpin in the pub and that was it. It was a good present though and I always remember Ruxpin's opening line, 'Hello, I hope we can be friends' – which seems to be a bit gay now. Another problem was that it feckin' ate the batteries. I had to steal four of the big oul' C types most days from the local shop to keep teddy talking.

HI, I AM TEDDY. I TELL STORIES AND SING SONGS, CHILDREN. FOLLOW YOUR NEW LEADER.

ROBOTS
WILL
RULE
THE
FUTURE

ACTION MAN

I had the proper Action Man with fuzzy hair, not that fake painted-on hair that they changed to. My Action Man could also move his eyes left and right with a little switch in the back of this head and he had a pull string to make him talk. I would think of all types of adventures for my doll. Some of these included: getting some rope and tying it to my bedroom window on the first floor and then tying the other end to the front gate, then sending Action Man down the 'zip-wire', just like Kevin McAllister did in Home Alone to get to his tree house; and tying a plastic bag to the doll and sending him out the first floor window to 'parachute' down (as my family would not buy me the proper parachuting Action Man). The one problem with the old-school fuzzy-haired Action Men was that they did not care too much for my extreme adventures. He would have needed an oul' trip to Advanced Hair Studios pretty quickly due to many, many concrete burns that caused many, many bald patches on his furry head.

THE AUTHOR'S INITIALS ARE AM (JUST LIKE THE LICENCE PLATES ON ACTION MAN CARS) AND HE HAS A SCAR IN THE EXACT SAME PLACE ON HIS CHEEK AS THE ACTION MAN DOLL, DUE TO THE REMOVAL OF A CYST WHEN HE WAS 7. HE THINKS THAT THIS IS COOL.

BARBIE VS SINDY

Most of my friends were fans of Sindy, but I was a Barbie girl. She had the small waist, big boobs and had the most handsome boyfriend in 'Ken'. I wanted to be her back then, but I want to be her even more now, as she is a bit heftier and slightly more realistic, the little ride! The makers changed the proportions in response to pressure from groups (thanks girls!) claiming Barbie's unrealistic proportions were a potential reason for the increase in teenage anorexia.

IN A SURVEY OF '80S KIDS, 46% OF GIRLS AGED 12 TO 14 CHECKED THEIR BROTHERS' ACTION MAN DOLLS IN THE HOPE OF SEEING WHAT THE HELL KIND OF PRIVATE PARTS A MAN HAD, WHILST 96% OF BOYS AGED 12 TO 14 USED TO SPEND TIME LOOKING AT THE BOOBIES OF THEIR SISTERS' BARBIE AND SINDY DOLLS.

FACT

FACT

Booty Camp

TRANSGENDER
DOLLS
NOW AVAILABLE

I can now be the doll I always wanted to be

Note:
Hands not included.

A PAWS FOR THOUGHT

OLD FOLKS, WANT TO SEE OUT YOUR FINAL DAYS WITH SOME SOFT LOVING CARE? THEN JOIN US AT

THE CARE BEAR RETIREMENT HOME

FACT

CARE BEARS & CARE BEAR COUSINS

Every girl's bedroom was full of Care Bear paraphernalia in the '80s. Mine was not just full of Funshine, Good Luck (the Irish Care Bear!), Cheer, Tenderheart, Friend, Wish, Bedtime and Love-A-Lot teddies (plus their cousins!!) with their plastic hearts from Care-A-Lot, their cloud home, it was also filled with Care Bear bedspreads, lamp shades, rugs, bean bags, etc. ♥

Remember the Care Bear message: love can conquer anything, and friends should stand side-by-side to help each other.

28% OF IRISH '80S BOYS AND GIRLS WHO LIKED THE CARE BEARS TURNED OUT TO BE HETEROSEXUAL.

♥ ♥

FECK IT
JUST OTHER BOY'S STUFF

G.I. JOE OFFICIALLY STANDS FOR
GOVERNMENT ISSUE JOE

FACT

CHUCK NORRIS KARATE KOMMANDOS

Chuck Norris Karate Kommandos were the business. When you squeezed the figure's legs, the fists would swing in a similar motion to Patrick Bergin in *Sleeping with the Enemy* (1991). ♥

CHUCK NORRIS TOOK A DAY TRIP TO LONGFORD; THAT'S WHY THE WHOLE COUNTY RESEMBLES A NUCLEAR HOLOCAUST.

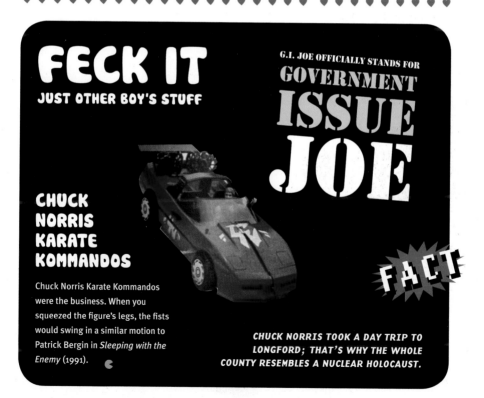

TOY TRACTORS

It did not matter if you were from West Mayo or Inner City Dublin, most boys had a pedal toy tractor. A Massey was the number one choice, but once it had a little trailer to carry around a few of your other toys, it did not really matter.

M.A.S.K. CARS

M.A.S.K. was one of my favourite cartoons and the toy cars were fantastic. I had the orange jeep with a switch on the side that would flip the car up and cause little machine guns to pop out. I think M.A.S.K. was shown early on a Saturday morning on BBC after The Racoons and before Grange Hill.

CHUTES AWAY!

Another cracking game! Chutes Away was advertised as an air-rescue game where you would drop weighted plastic chutes from a plane into craters that were on a rotating circular landscape below to 'rescue people'. I can tell you that every boy growing up playing this imagined that they were dropping big bombs on their worst enemy.

IF YOU ARE EVER IN A PLANE TRAVELLING A STEADY 210 MILES PER HOUR AT AN ALTITUDE OF 20,000 FEET AND WISH TO DROP A BOMB WEIGHING 250 LBS ON A SPECIFIC TARGET, YOU MUST DROP THAT BOMB 8.7 SECONDS BEFORE YOU FLY DIRECTLY ABOVE THAT MARK.

TOMY SUPER CUP ELECTRONIC FOOTBALL GAME

one of my aunts bought this game for my birthday. it was the best game I have ever owned, bar none. it would also eat the batteries but it did not matter, I would spend days playing it with anyone who would play against me. then one Tuesday night, my mother was out in Tomangoes and fell into the house locked. she stood on Tomy super cup and wrecked it. when I woke up the next morning I went looking for it, and eventually I woke her about 3pm, she told me she broke it and had thrown it out. she assured me that she would replace it. she never did.

FACT

SUBBUTEO

Subbuteo was a bit of a pain in the arse. The three flicks used to do my head in and the rules were always disputed. Then someone would stand on one of the players and you would have to superglue it back together, but it would never be the same.

JACK CHARLTON CONSIDERED USING SUBBUTEO IN THE 1990 WORLD CUP TO OUTLINE HIS TACTICS THE NIGHT BEFORE THE LAST 16 GAME AGAINST ROMANIA, UNTIL HE REALISED THAT EVERY PLAYER HAD THREE TOUCHES — THAT WAS TWO TOUCHES TOO MANY FOR HIM.

SCALEXTRIC

Loved this, and I can still remember that friction smell that you told everyone was 'burning rubber' from the track. A massive negative was the fact that every single time you went back and made a track after not using it for a while, you had to spend a few hours with sandpaper, sanding down the two metal strips that the cars run on.

SCALEXTRIC WAS OVERRATED, THERE WERE MUCH BETTER AND FASTER BRANDS. TOMY AFX VERTIGO WAS UNREAL.

FACT

TOP TIPS

DO NOT LEAVE YOUR TOMY SUPER CUP GAME ON THE SITTING ROOM FLOOR IF YOU KNOW YOUR MOTHER IS HEADING OUT ON SOCIAL WELFARE NIGHT TO TOMANGOES.

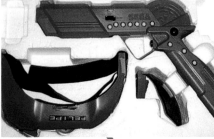

LAZER TAG/SEGA LOCK ON

Pretty much the coolest game at the time. Such was its popularity, it led to the establishment of Quasars in Leisureplexes around the country at the beginning of the '90s. Each Lazer Tag kit came with a gun, Star Belt, Star Vest and a Star Helmet. I felt like I could have been an army sniper, I was that good. And in fairness, you needed to be, in order to hit the sensor!!

BMX

can I start by saying that I thought the chopper was shite. The Brits have a huge hard-on for the chopper for some reason. BMXs were the only one for me. Myself and the gang would go around the estate in a convoy and put a plastic bottle at the back of the bike wheel to make it sound like a motor bike. I would then go and round up the smaller kids to lie down flat on the ground by threatening them with an unmerciful hidin'. I would then set up a concrete block on the ground with an oul' wooden board against it, beside the children. Myself and the lads would then 'attempt' to jump the kids. some of the other things that we got up to on our BMXs included:

seeing who could cram the most Kellogg's collectable reflectors into their spokes.

Taking bets on how many pedals you can do of a wheelie.

Taking bets on how many seconds you can go on your BMX with no hands.

Removing the brakes (because anyone who had brakes on their BMX was a homosexual).

THE FILM E.T. HELPED TO MAKE THE BMX POPULAR.

DIGITAL BIKE FROM THE FUTURE

RALEIGH VEKTAR

I had to include the Raleigh vektar. A god-awful 'futuristic' bike with an on-board computer. It really was horrendous. You were asking to be bullied cycling around on one of those.

ON-BOARD COMPUTER
THAT WAS ALWAYS BROKE.

OTHER GIRL'S STUFF

BIG YELLOW TEAPOT ♥

I loved doll houses and tea sets, so this was another perfect gift for me. You had Dad and Mam, a boy and two girls and a little dog in a very primitive house. A few nice little features included a slide for the family in the spout and a little roundabout in the lid!

BIG YELLOW TEAPOT IS WATERFORD SLANG FOR A GOLDEN SHOWER.

GLO WORMS

WARNING!! THIS TOY HAS BEEN DANGEROUS FOR YEARS. IN 2005, THE PRODUCT WAS FOUND TO HAVE A SUBSTANCE IN IT THAT COULD HARM CHILDREN. ITS PLASTIC HEAD IS SOFTENED WITH A DANGEROUS CHEMICAL AND CAN BE DANGEROUS IF SWALLOWED BY CHILDREN.

A LA CARTE KITCHEN & EASY-BAKE OVEN ♥

Remember the TV ad – 'Wake up Daddy, breakfast's ready' as some young one hands over a plastic bowl of baked beans on top of a Swiss Roll. It was the perfect present. I used to get chased out of the kitchen for 'helping' Mam with the dinner, so now I had my own kitchen to do whatever I liked. She would still go crazy when yogurts, real cutlery, bread and Jammy Dodgers would go missing from the real kitchen and appear in the cupboards of my A La Carte Kitchen.

It also had a sink, a cooker, and a fold-down table. However the cooker did not work so my next birthday present was the Easy-Bake Oven. I still cannot understand how a normal household light bulb could actually bake cakes. Dad always brought my Easy-Bake Oven cakes to work. Now that I think about it, I never actually saw him take a bite.

OVER 16 MILLION EASY-BAKE OVENS HAVE BEEN SOLD TO DATE AND IT HAS HELPED IN THE EDUCATION OF MANY HOUSEWIVES, SERVANTS AND SLAVES.

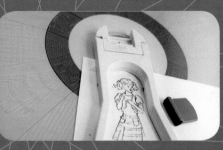

ELECTRONIC DREAM PHONE

Bruce was the hottest! Catherine Culleton started to cry when she got Phil one time (he was not a looker). A type of Guess Who game, you would get a boy's photo card and call the number on the electric phone. You would then listen to clues about your secret crush's favourite clothes, foods, positions, sports, etc., before trying to pick him out on the gameboard. If you thought you knew who the admirer was, then you made a special call to the boy's number and you would either hear 'You're right! I really like you!' or 'Urrgh, no way, I would not go feckin' near you.'

GIRLS, IF YOU EVER HAVE A CRUSH ON A BOY JUST TELL HIM. MOST LADS WOULD GET UP ON A CRACK BETWEEN TWO COUCH CUSHIONS, SO EVEN IF THE TIDE NORMALLY WOULDN'T TAKE YOU OUT, OFFER IT TO THE LAD ON A PLATE AND HE WILL DEFINITELY HAVE AT LEAST ONE NAKED LIE-DOWN CUDDLE WITH YOU.

TOP TIPS

FASHION WHEEL

I wanted to be a fashion designer after playing with Aileen O'Flaherty's Fashion Wheel on the last day of the school year when we were all allowed to bring in a toy. First you would rotate the outside circle to choose the bottom half of the design (mini-skirt, trousers, hold-ups, etc.), then rotate the middle circle to pick the top (jacket, t-shirt, diamante bra, etc.), and finally you would twist the inner circle to choose a head (short hair, long hair, mullet, etc.). The plastic frame would then be used to hold the circles in place as you rubbed your design out in colouring pencils or crayons.

NIALL ANTHONY USED FASHION WHEEL TO DESIGN HIS SPRING/ SUMMER RANGE OF '89.

FACT

SPIROGRAPH

Spirograph was a type of organised chaos. The 'creative kids' would claim it was a type of art and that you had to know about Spirograph and its techniques to fully understand and appreciate it. This group were bullied and bullied badly.

OTHER UNIVERSAL STUFF

LEGO

My brother and I had a huge bin full of mismatching Lego. We would spend hours upon hours making entire towns of Lego built with bricks of every colour of the rainbow. A life-sized version of the town would have attracted the likes of Louis Walsh, David Norris, Freddie Mercury and Joe Dolan.

THE ORIGINAL LEGO BLOCKS WERE MADE FROM WOOD AND HAD A FEW STUDS ON THE TOP AND A HOLLOW BOTTOM.

FACT

SWINGBALL

The loner's perfect game. If you were having hassle with the other boys in the area for getting caught and then 'squealing like a pig' on the gang's stash of bras and knickers that you all had stolen off the washing lines in the area over the previous 3 months, this was your game. The purchase of Swingball meant that Mam and Dad were happy enough that you were outside in the air playing (even if it was on your own) and then if the cousins came over they could play with you (until Bra and Knickergate blew over). The ball would zoom around at a ridiculous speed and if you stepped in too close, it would take your head off. The winner was whoever spun the ball enough for the string to reach the top or bottom of the coil.

TEENAGE MUTANT NINJA TURTLES AND REAL GHOSTBUSTERS

I was a massive Turtle fan; the inflatable Turtle blimp and the Michelangelo car that fired pizzas were great. I also had the four Ghostbusters: Ray Stantz, Egon Spengler, Winston Zeddmore, and Peter Venkman, plus their Ecto-1 car.

POGO BALLS OR LOLO BALLS

Two things stick in my mind with this contraption. Firstly, having really sore ankles from gripping the top part of the ball so hard. Secondly, I remember being absolutely knackered during a marathon pogo/lolo trip to the shop. Mam said, 'Don't bring that with you, you will be tired and fed up of it' and halfway there I realised she was right. Me being me, I would not give in and pogo-ed/lolo-ed through the pain and exhaustion barrier to the shops and then back home again.

ETCH A SKETCH

Another deeply frustrating device. By turning the two knobs a line would appear on the screen. One knob moved the line up and down while the other moved it left and right. Circles were impossible and to make a diagonal line, you had to move each knob a teeny tiny bit consecutively. If you made a mistake there was no way of correcting it, so you would shake the Etch a Sketch to clear the screen.

PLAY-DOH OR MALA/MARLA

IT IS A SMELL YOU WILL NEVER FORGET.

YOU WILL BE ABLE TO FIND BITS OF IT IN BEDROOM CARPETS ALL AROUND THE COUNTRY.

MOST KIDS MADE WILLIES AND BALLS AND NAKED WOMEN WITH BIG BOOBS MORE THAN ANY OTHER SHAPES.

YOU DID NOT DIE BY EATING MALA, BUT IT DID TASTE HORRIBLE AND SALTY FOR SOME REASON.

IF YOU MIX MALA COLOURS YOU CAN NEVER SEPARATE THEM AGAIN.

IF YOU LEAVE PLAY-DOH OUT OF ITS TUB OVERNIGHT, IT TURNS ROCK SOLID.

GET YOUR HANDS ON BROWN AND A TINY BIT OF BLACK MALA, MIX IT TOGETHER AND RUB A TINY BIT OF SAWDUST OR PENCIL PARINGS INTO THE CONCOCTION. PLACE IT ANYWHERE AND IT LOOKS LIKE A NICE LITTLE PILE OF SHITE.

RUN YOURSELF RAGGED / SCREWBALL SCRAMBLE

Another good one. A bunch of knobs, switches and buttons. Sixty seconds on the clock. You had to get the metal ball to traverse the wibbly wobbly bridge, swing on the magnet to the spreadable metal bars, cross the bars and crocodile pond, move across the uneven pad, down the bridge to the four jumpy log bits and through the hoop to the blind maze. You would wiggle the lever all over the shop to try and get the ball to come out (it was 50/50 whether it would come out the way it had gone in or the correct way!), then it was across on a swingy arrow thing to the arm that brings home the bacon and bangs the metal ball off the bell, thus allowing you to stop that timer!!

CHAPTER 6

THE TECHNOLOGY

Image: Otto – Vintage Toys

Though we may now look back and scoff at the slowness, pixelated-ness and all-round crap-ness of '80s technology, at the time, while we were proudly holding the orange Nintendo gun we felt we were standing on the cutting edge of technology and hoverboards were surely just around the corner. The amazing computers in Wall Street, the awe-inspiring control room in Top Gun and the sheer unbe-feckin'-lievable-ness of futuristic films like Total Recall was how we all thought the world would look by the year 2000. I remember watching Tomorrow's World and Beyond 2000 and being gobsmacked by the claims that a Compact Disc (CD) would take

over from the cassette. They reckoned that you could smear a CD with mayonnaise before drilling a hole in it and it would still play perfectly. So I put that to the test on my new Wham CD. The feckers!! Remember RTÉ's attempt at creating a new technology show on a shoestring budget? They famously reviewed a new range of piano neckties made from spandex! In this chapter we trawl through the essentials (the TV), the gadgets (Clarks Electric Foot Measuring Machine), the computers (Commodore 64), the computer games (Streets of Rage), the arcade games (Pac Man) and all the other indications that the pace of technological advancement in the '80s had reached Warp 8.

THE ESSENTIALS

THE TV

Ah, the aul' no remote TV. I had to get out of my chair to go over and change between RTÉ1, RTÉ2, BBC1, BBC2, UTV, and Channel 4. We were lucky to have six options, as many of my country bumpkin cousins only had the two RTÉ's until the mid-'90s. When we went on the holidays to our caravan (sorry, mobile home, mother!), we had a little black and white TV. When we wanted to watch The Den at 3pm, I would have to switch it on at 2.55pm to give it time to warm up and for the reception to clear.

INSUFFICENT FUNDS

ATM

The first ATM in Ireland was launched in 1980 and when I was very young, I thought that this was the most amazing thing ever. I could not get my head around putting in a card and getting a 'free' £20 out. I didn't fully understand that you could only get money out of the machine if you had money in the bank.

THE ABBREVIATION ATM IS ALSO USED BY PANASONIC TO IDENTIFY THEIR 4TH HIGHEST SELLING PRODUCT IN INDONESIA – THE ANUS TICKLING MACHINE

RECORDING MUSIC OFF THE RADIO ♥

I would get my old Fisher Price tape recorder or Home Alone 2 Talkboy and crouch beside my little radio every weekend to record the top 10. Fingers were poised to press the play and record buttons, and you would go feckin' nuts when the DJ cut the song early or even worse – talked over the end of the song!

THE COOLEST KID ON THE ROAD HAD RECORD LEVEL CONTROL ON HIS RECORDER, WHICH ENABLED HIM TO FADE OUT SONGS BEFORE THE DJ CUT IN TALKING. HIS TRACKS SOUNDED BRILLIANT AND HE USED TO GIVE SOME OF THEM TO PRETTY GIRLS TO LAY HIS FOUNDATIONS FOR FUTURE SHIFTING

PAY AND CALLCARD PHONES

It is very hard to even comprehend life without a mobile phone now. Imagine trying to meet a friend in town when you are both out and about already. A trip to the phonebox, a thumb through the business listings to find the regular haunts and a phone call to four or five pubs to see if he/she is there ... a right pain in the ass. Before the mobile, we had Telecom Éireann Pay and Callcard (from 1990 onwards) phones that were on every second street corner. It was very handy for prank calls and for calling out the fire brigade. I used to collect Callcards.

I remember asking Dad to stop off at a few Callcard phoneboxes in areas that I could not walk to, in the hope of finding a few used cards around the phone. I must have had about forty of the Tír na nÓg and Children of Lir editions as they were as common as half the cast of Fair City. I had a heap of the 5-Unit ones but never got my hands on the holy grail of the 100 Unit. There was a rumour that if you put a used callcard in the freezer overnight, it would gain a few units. This was absolute horseshit.

FACT

THERE ARE OFFICIAL EIRCOM CALLCARD COLLECTORS CLUBS. IN A SURVEY OF FIFTY MEMBERS, JUST THREE HAD FRIENDS OUTSIDE THE CALLCARD COLLECTORS CLUB.

THE GADGETS

WALKMAN PORTABLE CASSETTE PLAYER

This really changed the way we listened to music as you could listen to music anywhere you wanted for the first time. This meant that on long drives, you would not have to listen to Dad and Mam arguing, you would not have to play eye-spy with the rest of your saddo family, and you could listen to Jason and Kylie to drown out Dad's shite power ballads. The batteries would only last four or five hours, but thankfully we live on a small island and you could get to most places in that amount of time!

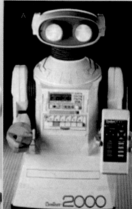

TOMY ROBOTS

In 1985, when I got my first Tomy Robot, I thought that by 1990 we would all have robot servants who would cater for all our daily needs. These little guys were remarkable for their time. I had the Tomy Omnibot which was a little fat robot with an annoying voice – think of Brian Dowling. Omnibot went forward and back, turned, ran on the carpet (this was a big deal), had great robot sound effects, blinking lights and could play tapes. You could also use the remote to talk through the robot and then your voice would sound robotic.

97

BIG TRAK

Big Trak was another one of the greatest '80s toys. I never had one but when a 'best friend' of mine (only because he had a Big Trak) got one off Santa, I cried with jealousy. The six-wheeler Big Trak could be programmed using a numbered keypad on the top-bed, and sent off to frighten the shite out of your little cousins with its flashing light or to deliver your empty glass and plate from dinner to the mother. To direct Big Trak, you would need to specify up to 16 directional steps, with instructions to turn a certain number of degrees (hopefully you had listened in that trigonometry lesson in Maths), pause, or move forward a certain distance.

BIG TRAK JR WAS LAUNCHED RECENTLY AND YOU CAN NOW ATTACH A DIGITAL CAMERA TO THE TOP, MAKING IT ABSOLUTELY PERFECT FOR PERVING ON SOME OF YOUR WIFE'S/HUSBAND'S OR GIRLFRIEND'S/ BOYFRIEND'S OR SISTER'S/BROTHER'S FRIENDS STAYING OVER IN YOUR PLACE.

FACT

DIGITAL WATCHES

At the beginning of the '80s, there was only one rich kid (his father owned the local chipper) in school who had a Casio digital watch. The little shit always seemed to have the newest and coolest gadgets, and he would make a big performance out of pressing the button so that the watch would light up. By the end of the decade, Casios were commonplace and some even featured a calculator (very handy in Maths!), a calendar and the famous TV remote control watch.

MR CASIO PRESENTED HIS FIRSTBORN SON WITH A GOLD WATCH ON HIS 16TH BIRTHDAY. SOME OF THE FEATURES INCLUDED A REMOTE CONTROL THAT ENABLED HIM TO 'PAUSE' CINEMA SCREENS, AN INBUILT ATM, A TRAFFIC LIGHT CHANGER, AND A CONDOM DISPENSER.

FACT

MOBILE PHONES

My first sighting of a 'mobile' phone was in the car park at Dublin Airport in the '80s. Some big Gordon Gekko wannabe was walking while holding what only can be described as a fridge freezer with his two hands and shouting into it. I also remember his rather attractive looking PA scurrying after him holding the battery box!

THE VCR

Again, it is pretty amazing to think about how amazed you were by a VCR back in the late '70s and '80s. You could now watch what you wanted (as long as the dodgy lad who came around the estate selling pirate videos had it in the boot of his car), when you wanted, and you could even watch the same thing over and over again. Before then, whatever was on the TV, you had to watch. My sister watched 9 to 5 (starring Jane Fonda, Lily Tomlin and Dolly Parton) so many times the video tape wore out. I also remember being truly stunned when I first saw that you could 'pause' an image on your TV. It was absolutely perfect for when the parents went out. 9 to 5 would be fast forwarded and then paused on Dolly!

Bamboozle!

Bamber Boozler poses another 12 questions. Answer using the fastext keys. One wrong and you must try again. Can you answer all 12 in one attempt?

Good day. Wow, I've just thought - less than two months to Christmas - crikey. Let's think no more and get into the questions.

Press RED to start

e-mail: bamboozle@teletext.co.uk

ARE YOU GETTING DEEPER INTO DEBT?
CALL MONEY TAILOR 08000 439922 p679

TELETEXT

TELETEXT was brilliant and it was the internet of the time for me. I still use it when I am in my Gran's house. Back in the '80s, TELETEXT was an added extra (£100 approx) if you were buying a TV and it was only included as standard in the '90s. Every single day, I would come home from school and check the football news on BBC page 302. Then on a Saturday, BBC page 303 would be on the TV from 3pm to 4.45pm to check the latest football scores. Also, during the week, I would play the Bamboozle quiz on Channel 4 on page 390, by pressing the green, blue, red and yellow buttons (nobody knew what they were for) on the remote control.

THE TECHNOLOGY TO ROLL OUT AERTEL WAS AVAILABLE TO RTÉ SINCE 1973, HOWEVER THE CATHOLIC CHURCH BANNED THEM FROM DOING SO.

FACT

IN A SURVEY OF 100 IRISH COMMODORE 64 OWNERS, 73% ARE NOW EMPLOYED AS ACCOUNTANTS OR WORK IN THE TAX OFFICE.

FACT

CLARKS ELECTRIC FOOT MEASURING MACHINE

This was very scary and completely pointless. You would be hauled into the Clarks shop at the end of August and made to stand on a machine to measure your shoe size for the coming school year (and the following one). No matter what size you were, your mother would add two sizes anyway (See the Clothes and Accessories chapter). While you were on the machine, a heavy metal bar would come down to measure your feet. I remember nearly weeing myself as I thought it was going to crush my feet.

THE COMPUTERS

CRAPPY HANDHELD COMPUTER GAMES

There really were a lot of these in the '80s and early '90s. Most were football, American football or basketball themed (it really didn't matter as the gameplay was the exact same), had a few basic buttons and made a very annoying 'beep' after every single move or play. Then the Nintendo Game and Watch came on the scene. I had the Donkey Kong version and this was pretty good. The object was to save a girl from a big bold monkey.

COMMODORE 64

This was fairly crap. My lasting memory is sitting in my cousin's house waiting ages for the cassettes to load and the bleedin' counter turning ever so slowly. Some of the half-decent games were Flimbo's Quest, Paperboy and Gauntlet.

99

ZX Spectrum+
Personal Computer

ZX SPECTRUM

THE ZX SPECTRUM IS KNOWN AS THE 'SPECCY' BY I.T. FANS. IN A SURVEY OF GAMERS WHO STILL RATHER AFFECTIONATELY REFER TO IT AS SPECCY, 87% LIVE WITH THEIR MOTHERS, HAVE BEARDS AND A PONYTAIL AND MASTURBATE ABOUT LARA CROFT (NOT THE ANGELINA JOLIE VERSION AS SHE IS NOT PERFECT ENOUGH).

FACT

GAMEBOY

FACT

THE TECHNOLOGY CONTAINED IN A SINGLE GAME BOY UNIT IN THE YEAR 1990 EXCEEDED ALL THE COMPUTING POWER USED TO PUT THE FIRST MAN ON MOON IN 1969.

NINTENDO

I got this from Santa the first Christmas it came out, and I thought I was the shit. What a computer! It was just a simple grey box with two buttons on the front and a flip-up lid where you would slide a game in and push it down. Looking at the rectangular controllers now, they look ridiculously basic.

BARCODE BATTLER

Probably the worst handheld game ever and had absolutely brutal graphics. You would get a set of cards, each with a barcode, and you would battle with friends to see whose barcode had the best 'power' or 'strength' … Yep, it really was as crap as it sounds.

THE BARCODE BATTLER STAGED A COMEBACK IN THE MID-NOUGHTIES, HOWEVER IT RETURNED IN THE FORM OF MY FRIEND (A LUKE KELLY FAN), WHO USED TO GET INTO A FIGHTS EVERY WEEK IN BARCODE NIGHTCLUB, CLONTARF, DUBLIN.

'I wouldn't say I was the best manager in the business. But I was in the top one.' **Brian Clough**

MEGADRIVE VERSUS SUPER NINTENDO

There used to be fisticuffs in my schoolyard between Megadrive and Super Nintendo owners. Both would give their reasons why they thought their console was better, and then I would decide that the Megadrive was better – as I had one at home. You would turn it on and here the famous 'segaaaaaaaaaaaa'. I remember having a few lads over for a FIFA 95 tournament. We all picked different teams and set up a world cup. I somehow lost in the first round and I was not a happy camper to say the least, considering it was my house. Being the experienced Megadrive player, I knew that if something bumped off the console, it would freeze and the game would have to be reset. So I asked Jason Gannon if he wanted to have a game of 'slaps' right beside the Megadrive. I hit him so hard that he fell into the computer and it 'unfortunately' froze, which resulted in us having to start the tournament all over again. I then won it.

THE COMPUTER GAMES

FIRST DIVISION MANAGER

You can keep your Championship and Football Managers, First Division Manager on the Atari was the business. It was probably the first real game of this type and you could buy the likes of Quinn, Stapleton, Gazza and Chris Morris. It was pretty detailed; you could train your players, fire the assistant manager and even discuss loans to buy players with the bank manager.

MOST MALE '80S KIDS HAVE LOST WEEKS, MONTHS AND EVEN YEARS OF THEIR LIFE TO CHAMPIONSHIP AND FOOTBALL MANAGER.

© 1991 SEGA
MUSIC © 1991 YUZO KOSHIRO

STREETS
OF RAGE

My favourite 'beat 'em up', just ahead of 'Double Dragon' and 'Street Fighter'.

This Megadrive game was class and I would spend hours beating up hundreds of identical baddies in blue (one punch or kick would kill these) and red (it took three good smacks to kill the reds) sweatshirts.

There was a great story to the game too. Axel, Blaze, and Max had quit the corrupt police force to become vigilantes, in order to defeat the crime lord Hawk. 'What was once a happy, peaceful, productive city, full of life and activity, has fallen into the hands of a secret criminal syndicate. Looting, random violence and destruction are rampant. No one is safe walking the streets, day or night...'. Think of Limerick City now, and you should have an idea.

The thing that most people remember is that Streets of Rage had two possible endings. In one player mode, you defeated Hawk at the end and completed the game. However, in two player mode, Hawk asks you both to join his crime syndicate and the big thing was that one of the players HAD to join him!!!

And then you had to fight it out with each other! If the player who joined Hawk wins, you then had to fight him and if successful you became the new crime boss. If this happens the screen then says 'If the player who became the 'Bad Guy' wins, he has to fight the boss. If successful he is then the new Boss! The screen then shows the words 'You are great! You are the new Boss!' and your character can then be heard doing an evil laugh before the final words of 'Bad Ending' appear on the screen. I thought this was feckin' brilliant!

HIGH SCORE   YOUR SCORE
000000   000000

F1 BEGINNER   F3 ADVANCED   F5 SUICIDAL

```
Amstrad 128K Microcomputer   (v3)
©1985 Amstrad Consumer Electronics plc
          and Locomotive Software Ltd.
BASIC 1.1
Ready
■
```

Prepare to wait for ages for your game to load.
Sometimes the graphics are not as impressive as the
images on the back of the cassette box that you bought
in your local games shop for around five pounds.

SONIC

Sega's rival to Nintendo's Mario. I can still hear the jingle of the gold coins when they hit the ground and remember the excitement of turning into a ball on a downslope as Sonic.

SONIC WAS ORIGINALLY ENTITLED 'MR NEEDLEMOUSE' (THE JAPANESE WORD FOR HEDGEHOG).

SEGA
MEGA DRIVE
670-3620-50

SUPER MARIO AND DUCK HUNT WITH THE ORANGE GUN

Super Mario Brothers was a global smash hit for Nintendo. It was the first game that seemed to have truly universal appeal. I do not know one person who didn't like Mario, his super mushrooms and how he went into a little castle and raised a flag at the end of each level.

Duck Hunt, with its pretty snazzy orange light gun, usually came with the Nintendo and Mario. It was great that the whole family could have a go (similar to when the Wii first came out). I remember my Granny standing in the middle of the room at Christmas shooting ducks and cursing at the dog on the screen for laughing at her when she missed her targets.

THE IRISH ARMY PURCHASED A BULK SHIPMENT OF NINTENDOS WITH DUCK HUNT IN 1989 TO FORM PART OF A NEW WEAPONS TRAINING PROGRAMME.

THE ARCADE GAMES

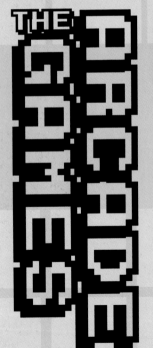

BLANKA ANGRY

STREET FIGHTER

This was the classic arcade game and far better than the console versions of the late '80s and '90s. On one-player mode, you were Ryu, or if your friend was playing, he was Ken and you competed in a worldwide martial arts tournament, spanning five countries and ten opponents. You had one button for punch and one for kick and the harder you hit the buttons the harder Ryu and Ken would hit (or so we thought)!

AS STREET FIGHTER GAINED POPULARITY THROUGHOUT THE '80S, AN UNDERGROUND REAL-LIFE VERSION OF THE GAME DEVELOPED LEGS IN THE MEAN STREETS OF PORTARLINGTON. THE GARDAÍ FINALLY GOT THINGS UNDER CONTROL WHEN LEGO MCGURK WAS ADMITTED TO HOSPITAL AFTER BEING HIT BY CHI-BLAST (A LEATHER FOOTBALL THAT HAD BEEN DOSED IN PETROL AND SET ALIGHT) RELEASED BY SPUD MAHONY.

SPACE INVADERS

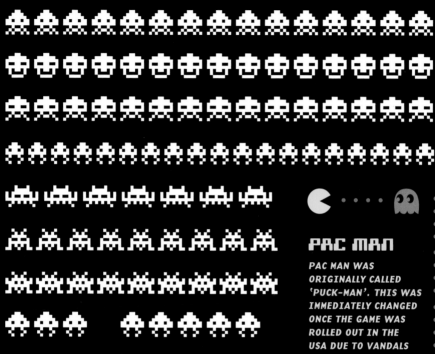

PAC MAN

PAC MAN WAS
ORIGINALLY CALLED
'PUCK-MAN'. THIS WAS
IMMEDIATELY CHANGED
ONCE THE GAME WAS
ROLLED OUT IN THE
USA DUE TO VANDALS
SCRATCHING OUT PART
OF THE 'P'.

SPACE INVADERS IS RANKED
AS THE TOP ARCADE GAME BY
THE GUINNESS WORLD RECORDS.

CHAPTER 7

THE TV SHOWS + FILMS

If you lived in the serious shticks growing up, you mightn't remember all of the TV programmes here, just the dodgy Irish ones and the ones cheap enough for RTÉ to import. Dubs, of course, had all the channels – the BBCs, ITV and Channel 4 – and so they are better-rounded, highly cultured intellectuals, because they would watch the highbrow likes of Bullseye, Baywatch and Supermarket Sweep. Everyone should remember the movies mentioned though, and if there are any you haven't seen you should sort that out because they're all classics. Back in the '80s, most of our movies were purchased from dodgy men with ponytails in markets or from a guy who would drive around selling pirate tapes from the boot of his car (along with bottles of American Cream Soda, for some reason). The odd week, we'd make the trip to the video shop for a decent version of a film that we really wanted to see. Please REWIND the video tape before returning it.

TELLY

MADE IN ENGLAND

There were plenty of classic English TV programmes that could have been mentioned, and in my Granddad's humble opinion, the Brits excelled at quiz shows.

BULLSEYE

The famous character 'Bully' was ambidextrous. At the opening of the show he was shown to throw darts with his right hand, however prior to the advert break midway through the show, he can be seen to write 'End of part one' using his left hand. Also, the legendary 'TV with wired remote control' prize on the programme has regularly been voted as one of the worst ever TV game show prizes.

CRYSTAL MAZE

The custom-built maze was the largest purpose-built game show set in the world in 1990, costing in the region of £250,000 and it was approximately the size of two football pitches. Legendary bald presenter Richard O'Brien also wrote the Rocky Horror Picture Show, has been married twice and has fathered three children.

GOING FOR GOLD

'GOING FOR GOLD! THE HEAT IS ON, THE TIME IS RIGHT, IT'S TIME FOR YOU, FOR YOU TO PLAY YOUR GAMES. 'CAUSE PEOPLE ARE COMING, EVERYONE'S TRYING, TRYING TO BE THE BEST THAT THEY CAN, WHEN THEY'RE GOING FOR ... GOING FOR ... GOLD.

The famous Going for Gold Theme tune was composed by none other than Hans Zimmer, the multiple Oscar, Golden Globe and Grammy award-winning score composer of The Lion King, Gladiator, Crimson Tide, Inception and The Dark Knight.

SUPERMARKET SWEEP

'The next time you're at the checkout and you hear the beep (bip-bip), think of the fun you could be having on Supermarket Sweeeeep!'

In a survey of 100 Irish '80s Kids entitled, 'What was your favourite inflatable bonus from Supermarket Sweep?', the results were; BANANA 46%, GUITAR 23%, DOLL 17% AND SHEEP 14%.

15 TO 1

The introduction credits on one show featured a contestant called Carl Majors from Ilfracombe, who famously listed his profession as a 'Fudge Packer'.

MADE IN IRELAND

MAKE AND DO

Make and Do producers courted controversy in 1987 when they insisted that presenter Mary FitzGerald made a scale model of 6 foot by 2 foot wooden plank on the show. Mary was not one bit happy as she considered Pat Kenny a good friend.

THAT'S BLEEDIN' RAPID

PHYSIQUIZ

Kevo 'Bleedin' Rapid' was the presenter of this RTÉ show where contestants would throw frisbees into gaps and balls at a Velcro wall. Kevo 'Bleedin' Rapid' also appears in The Sex/Shift/Wear/Score/Meet Symbols chapter.

ZOGA BONGS

SCRATCH SATURDAY

In a survey of 100 Irish '80s Kids entitled 'Who had the most annoying voice on Irish TV in the '80s?', Scratch Saturday presenter Mary 'Are you laughing?' Kingston topped the vote with a massive 94%.

JO MAXI

In Ireland, the term 'Jo Maxi' is rhyming slang for a 'taxi'. In New Zealand, the infamous Jo Maxi was arrested for the act of necrophilia towards animals in 1989 after he had murdered 387 sheep over the course of a three-year period.

KNOW YOUR SPORT

Memory Man Jimmy Magee was a legend and the best part about this programme. However, isn't it strange that the Memory Man cannot correctly name half of today's football players but can recall the Olympic Bantamweight (54kg) Boxing Champion, Wolfgang Behrendt, from 1956.

THE DEN

In a survey of 100 Irish '80s Kids entitled 'Who was the best presenter on The Den?', the results were:

IAN DEMPSEY	65%
DAMIEN McCAUL	15%
FRANCIS BOYLAN JR	12%
KATHRYN McKIERNAN	7%
RAY D'ARCY	1%

HEAD 2 TOE

It was most secondary school kids' dream for RTÉ's Head 2 Toe to come to their school and revamp their crappy uniform.

WHERE IN THE WORLD?
'PASS, AFRICA 6'

Theresa Lowe (please see The Sex/Shift/Wear/Score/Meet Symbols chapter), was the only reason my Granddad, Uncles, Brother, Aunt Mary and myself, watched Where in the World?

MILEY

GLENROE

88% of '80s boys and girls surveyed used to pretend to be interested in what Miley, Biddy, Dinny, Blackie and that home-wrecker Fidelma were up to in Glenroe on a Sunday night, in order to stay up later.

OTHERS:

YOUNGLINE
MURPHY'S MICRO QUIZ
TALKABOUT
ACTION STATION SATURDAY
PAJO'S JUNKBOX

JUDGE MENTAL

WANDERLY WAGON

Most people born in the '70s have memories of eating their fry while watching Wanderly Wagon on a Saturday evening.

CON FER

GENDER-LESS BOSCO IS A BOY!

ON 9 MAY 2011 ON A WELL-KNOWN NATIONWIDE RADIO SHOW, BOSCO LET SLIP THAT HE IS A BOY, SAYING THAT THEY KEPT HIS GENDER A SECRET FOR 33 YEARS.

MADE IN USA, CANADA OR AUSTRALIIA

CLOSER EACH DAY

MURDER SHE WROTE

Every day the author's Granny would take an hour off from her daily chores of washing, ironing, scrubbing floors, peeling spuds, dropping other aul' ones to Mass in her Mini, etc., to sit down and see what her idol Jessica Fletcher was up to in Cabot Cove.

ROSEANNE

The TV show's original title was 'Life and Stuff'. George Clooney appeared in season one, as Roseanne's boss at work, and in the early years of the show there was a naked picture of Gorgeous George on a fridge on set. This photo was allegedly taken by Roseanne herself or John Goodman when the three of them went out on a booze-filled session.

HOME AND AWAY/ NEIGHBOURS

The streets would noticeably clear of girls and a hell of a lot of boys for the hour that Neighbours and Home and Away were on. Was this because it coincided with dinner

MORK AND MINDY

Mork and Mindy was a spinoff of Happy Days! The character Mork (Robin Williams) first appeared in Happy Days, where he attempts to kidnap Richie and bring him back to Ork as a human specimen. Fonzie foils this plan but it al turns out to be Richie's dream anyway! Williams' character was so popular that he got his own series - Mork & Mindy.

STAR TREK: THE NEXT GENERATION

STAR TREKKIN' ACROSS THE UNIVERSE,
ON THE STARSHIP ENTERPRISE
UNDER CAPTAIN KIRK.
STAR TREKKIN' ACROSS THE UNIVERSE,
ONLY GOING FORWARD 'CAUSE
WE CAN'T FIND REVERSE.

There have been some very famous gues appearances on The Next Generation: Kirsten Dunst (Hedril), Kelsey Grammer (Captain Morgan Bateson), Teri Hatcher (Lt. Bronwyn Gail Robinson), Stephen Hawking (Middle Distance Athlete at Space Olympics), and Ashley Judd

SAVED BY THE BELL

In a survey of 100 Irish female '80s Kids entitled 'Who did you fancy the most in Saved by the Bell?', Zack Morris 51%, A.C. Slater 44%, Kelly Kapowski 4% and Mr Belding 1%, were the results.

BAYWATCH

Baywatch was the most watched TV show of all time, with over 1.1 billion weekly viewers around the world, according to the Guinness Book of World Records.

ALIEN LIFE FORM

The friendly extraterrestrial whose nickname is an acronym for Alien Life Form. Also, Alf has eight stomachs, his heart is located in his head, he is circumcised and he eats cats.

WWF

In a survey of 100 Irish '80s Kids, 63% voted Brett 'the Hitman' Heart as their favourite wrestler ever.

FRAGGLE ROCK

DANCE YOUR CARES AWAY
WORRIES FOR ANOTHER DAY
LET THE MUSIC PLAY
DOWN AT FRAGGLE ROCK

WORK YOUR CARES AWAY
DANCING'S FOR ANOTHER DAY
LET THE FRAGGLES PLAY
WE'RE GOBO, MOKEY
WEMBLEY, BOOBER, RED

DANCE YOUR CARES AWAY
WORRIES FOR ANOTHER DAY
LET THE MUSIC PLAY
DOWN AT FRAGGLE ROCK
DOWN AT FRAGGLE ROCK
DOWN AT FRAGGLE ROCK

MACHO MAN RANDY SAVAGE

RIP

QUANTUM LEAP

The main character, Sam was involved in a number of significant historical events through various 'Leaps'.

He demonstrates a moonwalk to a young black kid called Michael.

He has sexual relations with a young curvaceous woman called Ms Lewinsky on top of a table in an office that is oval in shape.

He performs a manoeuvre on a choking man called Dr Heimlich.

He advises an inebriated jilted wife (a lady with a name that rhymes with Blink) to call and leave a message on her ex-husband's phone, telling him to 'zip up his little man', amongst other things.

He advises a 12 year old called Trump that investing in New York City real estate would be a good way to get rich.

He helps a young Chubby Checker to do 'The Twist'.

THE WONDER YEARS

In a survey of 100 Irish '80s Kids, 29% voted The Wonder Years 'With a Little Help from My Friends', as their favourite theme tune ever. This song was originally written by Paul McCarthy, with input by John Lennon, for Ringo Starr. Joe Cocker performs the version of the song that is used on The Wonder Years.

'What would you do if I sang out tune? Would you stand up and walk out on me?'

LOVE BOAT

74% of '80s boys and girls surveyed thought that they were somehow being naughty by sneakily watching 'The Love Boat'.

CHiPs

Ponch and Jon were Californian Highway Patrolmen (CHP), hence the name CHiPs. The roads of California are the most dangerous in the world, as every Saturday teatime there was a huge multi-car freeway pile-up for the CHiPS boys to deal with.

OFFICER
FRANCIS
LLEWELLYN
"PONCH"

HANDY

MacGYVER

MacGyver actor Richard Dean Anderson admitted in an interview on a late-night chatshow that he once convinced a dim-witted lady fan of the show (back at his home) that he was trained to improvise and troubleshoot all problems by using ordinary household items. He then put a used bag of Manhattan Popcorn, Fairy Liquid and an elastic band to good use.

OTHERS:

COSBY SHOW
KUNG FU
THE A-TEAM
REMINGTON STEELE
JAKE AND THE FAT MAN
DALLAS
THE BRADY BUNCH
HAPPY DAYS
LITTLE HOUSE ON THE PRAIRIE
SESAME STREET
THE LITTLEST HOBO
AIRWOLF

NITELINK RIDER

MICHAEL, YOU APPEAR TO HAVE FALLEN ASLEEP ON THE NITELINK AGAIN. YOU ARE NOW IN BALBRIGGAN. GOOD LUCK.

NIGHT RIDER

Hasselhoff's car, 'KITT' is an acronym for Knight Industries Two Thousand.

CARTOONS

DOGTANIAN AND THE THREE MUSKEHOUNDS

At the end of season two, the Three Muskehounds (Porthos, Athos and Aramis) had a massive 'falling out' with Dogtanian and the producers of the programme. They felt that Dogtanian was getting preferential treatment (he was allowed to give any of the 'extras' a bone) and that his deal on image rights was far superior to theirs.

CARE BEARS

28% of Irish '80s boys and girls who liked the Care Bears turned out to be heterosexual.

MUPPET BABIES

Talks are underway in the UK to secure the future children of the cast of The Only Way is Essex and Geordie Shore for a reality show entitled Muppet Babies.

CAPTAIN PLANET

Captain Planet was ahead of its time and attempted to educate the next generation on a variety of environmental issues. However, when we would play Captain Planet on the road using penny jelly rings, nobody wanted to be left with 'Heart', so we would all quickly bagsy Earth, Fire, Wind and Water!

TEENAGE MUTANT NINJA TURTLES (TMNT)

'COWABUNGA.'
When TMNT arrived in Ireland and the UK in the '80s, the name was changed to 'Teenage Mutant Hero Turtles', because censorship authorities deemed the word 'ninja' to have excessively violent connotations for a children's programme.

INSPECTOR GADGET

'WOWSERS!'
The 1999 live-action Disney film version starring Matthew Broderick as Gadget and Rupert Everett as Doctor Claw was absolutely shite.

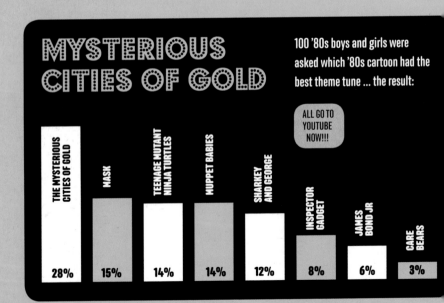

MYSTERIOUS CITIES OF GOLD

100 '80s boys and girls were asked which '80s cartoon had the best theme tune ... the result:

ALL GO TO YOUTUBE NOW!!!

THE MYSTERIOUS CITIES OF GOLD	MASK	TEENAGE MUTANT NINJA TURTLES	MUPPET BABIES	SHARKEY AND GEORGE	INSPECTOR GADGET	JAMES BOND JR	CARE BEARS
28%	15%	14%	14%	12%	8%	6%	3%

TEENAGE MUTANT NINJA TURTLES

JAMES BOND JR

BOND
JAMES BOND JUNIOR
NO-ONE CAN STOP HIM, BUT SCUM
ALWAYS TRIES
YOUNG BOND CUTS THROUGH
EACH WEB OF SPIES
HE LEARNED THE GAME FROM
HIS UNCLE JAMES
NOW HE'S HEIR TO THE NAME –
JAMES BOND.

(BOND, JAMES BOND JR)
LOOK OUT HE'S COMIN' THROUGH,
HE'S GOTTA JOB TO DO,
WHILE HE RESCUES THE GIRL,
JAMES BOND JR CHASES S.C.U.M.,
(JAMES BOND JR CHASES S.C.U.M.)
AROUND THE WORLD.

This was the best cartoon ever made.

OTHERS:

MASK
THUNDERCATS
SMURFS
THE RACCOONS

BY THE POWER OF GREYSKULL

HE-MAN

Due to strict broadcasting standards in cartoons of the '80s, He-Man was not allowed to use his sword as an offensive weapon, he was not allowed to punch or kick anyone and he could only destroy robotic enemies.

MY TOP FILMS

IN' A SHAR'N'

THE COMMITMENTS

This was most culchies' first insight into Dublin life.

ROXANNE

A replica of the Steve Martin character, C.D. Bale's nose from the 1987 film Roxanne, was the 4th highest-selling unofficial sex toy in Connacht in 1988.

3 MEN AND A BABY

Ted Danson 14%, Steve Guttenberg 31% and Tom Selleck 55%, were the survey results of 100 Irish women when asked, which character would they now fancy the most from the 1987 hit 3 Men and a Baby.

THE GREMLINS

It is one of those films that most people watch around Christmas time. Also, the talking teddy 'Furby' was considered so similar to the character Gizmo that the film production company considered a lawsuit.

HOME ALONE

'KEEP THE CHANGE YOU FILTHY ANIMAL.' The infamous 'Angels with Filthy Souls' scene of the gangster with a 'tommy gun' shooting some schmuck, shown by Kevin to scare the pizza-boy away, is a fictional gangster film and was made especially for Home Alone.

KARATE KID

One of the Cobra Kai (the baddies) is played by Chad McQueen, son of Steve McQueen.

THE GOONIES

The number of times a Goonies character says the word 'shit' or 'bullshit' is nineteen, not counting the line 'Holy shit!' Most '80s Kids thought that this was really bold.

GIZMO

THE BREAKFAST CLUB

John Bender (Judd Nelson) is the worst name for a movie badass in the long history of film. Also, Molly Ringwald was extremely overrated and does not deserve the frequent title of 'The Greatest Teen Star of All Time'.

JAWS

The author's uncle was on a family holiday in Wexford during the '80s. Two of his sisters were in the sea swimming as he waded out to them (he cannot swim but according to himself, he 'can hold his breath for a long time') in chest-high water. He started to hum the famous Jaws 'shark' theme ... dum dun, dum dun, dum dun ... in order to frighten the girls. Next thing, the two ladies spotted my uncle running back towards the sand, looking scared and panicking. Eventually the two finished swimming and headed back to their towels and to my uncle, where he admits that he had frightened the shite out of himself by humming the tune!

BABY GETS NOSE SHAVE

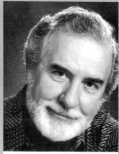

BEFORE   **AFTER**

DIRTY DANCING

Main female lead, Jennifer Grey, had a 'nose-job' in the early '90s, which changed her nose and made her face almost unrecognisable from her 'Baby' character. She was not able to take advantage of her success in Dirty Dancing, as most film directors did not recognise her initially and they felt that the public would not be able to tell it was 'Baby' either!

FLUX CAPACITOR

BACK TO THE FUTURE

A great film quote: Biff Tannen (Back to the Future, 1985): 'I have your car towed all the way to your house and all you've got for me is *lite* beer?'

79% of '80s Kids surveyed thought that we would have been zooming around on Hoverboards by now when they watched Back to the Future II in 1989.

FERRIS BUELLER'S DAY OFF

Matthew Broderick (Ferris) and Jennifer Grey (Jeanie) played brother and sister in the film, but were jaunting at the time it was made.

GHOSTBUSTERS

The original title was Ghost Smashers and Eddie Murphy was originally planned to star as Winston.

OTHERS:

STAR WARS

ROCKY

GHOST

STAND BY ME

SUPERMAN

TOP GUN

THE SNAPPER

CHAPTER 8

THE SEX / SHIFT / WEAR / SCORE / MEET SYMBOLS

WARNING: There will be disputes over this chapter. I think it's fair to say that when Irish kids were growing up, we (or certainly I) didn't know what sex was until about age 12. To call this chapter 'The Sex Symbols', therefore, just didn't feel right. When we were in the pre-teens, we knew that we would love to do something to Larry Mullen Jr or Roxette, but we were not really certain what that was! So most of the time, we just imagined 'shifting', 'wearing the face off', 'scoring' or 'meeting them' – depending on which part of the country you were from. We surveyed 1,000 non-imaginary male and female Irish '80s Kids and the results, as verified by Dermot Whelan himself, are bound to generate debate, featuring as they do, Hollywood hotties, one priest (come on down, Fr Sinead O'Connor!) and some men with just lovely blow-dried hair. Allow us to present the Top 10 Irish Males, Irish Females, International Males and International Females that you'd like to, you know … do something to.

IRISH FEMALE TOP TEN

1. ALISON DOODY

Alison was and still is an absolute ride. If you ever want to meet up sometime for a coffee and a shift Alison, please give me a call on 087-ILOVEDOODYS.

2. THERESA LOWE

Theresa is now a top barrister and she is married to Frank McNamara (the man who played the piano on most of the *Late Lates* when Gaybo was still around).

3. SINEAD O'CONNOR

Sinead famously tore up a picture of the Pope on *Saturday Night Live*, in front of a nationwide American audience in 1992. However, it was a huge mistake. She was going through one of her 'mad at the world' episodes and had really intended to tear up a picture of herself to symbolise 'the disposable nature of an upper middle class, self absorbed, self-obsessed, do anything controversial just to be controversial, big child', but unfortunately Sinead had left her contact lenses in her hotel room. She inadvertently picked up her assistant druid's picture of a baldish, plumpish, hero that was dressed in virginal white and assumed it was herself.

4. ANGELINE BALL

Angeline was a little stunner. I would have used her shite as toothpaste.

5. MARIA DOYLE KENNEDY

Maria came a close second (48%) to Angeline Ball (52%) in a survey of 100 Irish '80s boys, when asked 'Which of the three Commitments backing singers did you fancy the most?' The other one unfortunately failed to register.

6. CYNTHIA NÍ MHURCHÚ

'Get it inte ye' Cynthia is also a top barrister in the Four Courts. The highlight of her RTÉ career was presenting the 1994 Eurovision with the late, great Gerry Ryan. It is still so hard to believe that Gerry is gone (sniff, sniff) and I really miss his gravelly, 'come to bed and I'll ride ya' voice in the mornings.

7. SANDY KELLY

64% of '80s boys from the counties of Mayo, Sligo and Donegal surveyed put country legend Sandy Kelly as their number one '80s Sex Symbol.

8 / 9 / 10. MIRIAM O'CALLAGHAN / MARY KENNEDY / ANNE DOYLE

The survey suggests that Miriam, Mary and Anne were average enough Sex/Shift/Wear/Score/Meet Symbols during the '80s. However, all three are now considered to be MILF and GILF-tastic.

OTHER SEXY MINXES

SHAUNA LOWRY
MICHELLE ROCCA
MARY BLACK
MARY KINGSTON

IRISH MALE TOP TEN

IRISH·MALE TOP TEN

1. LARRY MULLEN JR

Larry Jr's hair naturally produces its own styling gel.

2. PIERCE BROSNAN

Pierce, Ringo Starr and Alec Baldwin have all made appearances as narrators on *Thomas the Tank Engine*.

3. GABRIEL BYRNE

Gabriel wanted to become a priest, but he was thrown out of the seminary after getting caught smoking in a cemetery.

4. DANIEL O'DONNELL

Daniel has wonderful hair, a happy outlook on life, enjoys herbal cigarettes and sambuca (never at the same time), and long strolls around deserted car parks at night.

5. DANIEL DAY-LEWIS

After his Oscar-winning performance as Christy Brown, Daniel played the lead role in a National Theatre production of *Hamlet*. At the beginning of the run, he collapsed in the middle of the scene where the ghost of Hamlet's father first appears to his son. Daniel began sobbing uncontrollably and refused to go back on stage. Although the incident was officially attributed to exhaustion, Day-Lewis later confirmed on *Parkinson* that he had seen the ghost of his own father and he has not appeared on stage ever since.

6. PACKIE BONNER

78% of '80s girls surveyed from the Leinster region (they love the Donegal accent for some reason) placed Packie Bonner as their number 1 Irish '80s Sex Symbol. However, he failed to score a single vote in his home province of Ulster, which brought him down to 6th place.

7. KEVIN O'CONNELL

(KEV/KEVO/'BLEEDIN' RAPID' GUY) FROM RTÉ SATURDAY MORNING TV.
Kevo is the illegitimate lovechild of Bella from Fair City and Teasy from Glenroe. Soon after his birth, RTÉ legally adopted him under the same legislation the major television network in the US used to snare Truman Burbank. He was first put to work reading 'buuks' on the toy show and then RTÉ decided to move him onto such classics as Physiquiz (where the other presenter was Barry Murphy of Aprés Match fame), Scratch Saturday, The Works, Iota and Quiz Stream.

8. JOHNNY LOGAN

Johnny rarely speaks to the Irish press, due to frequent misquotes in the media. He kindly said the following when contacted about his inclusion at number 8 in this list of Irish sex symbols, 'What the **** do you mean that Daniel O' ****ing Donnell and Packie ****ing Bonner are ahead of me on the ****ing list. Women all over the ****ing world love me. I am a big ****ing deal. I won the ****ing Eurovision twice on my ****ing own and an even bigger achievement was winning it with a ****ing song I wrote for Linda ****ing Martin because she is ****ing brutal ...' (then he hung up).

9. MICHAEL LYSTER

While on holiday in Florida in his younger days, Michael was repeatedly tormented for his autograph by the American public. They thought he was a young Judge Reinhold.

10. DERMOT WHELAN

26% of Irish '80s girls surveyed, chose Dermot as their number one, when they were asked to pick one current Irish stand-up comedian they reckoned would have been a decent shift back in the '80s. It was a closely run contest and he just pipped Neil Delamere, Tommy Tiernan and Katherine Lynch.

OTHER SEXY BEASTS

AONGHUS McANALLY
PAUL McGRATH
JOHN ALDRIDGE
EAMONN COGHLAN
KEVIN SHARKEY
JOHNNY LOGAN
FERGAL SHARKEY
PAT KENNY
MARTY WHELAN

INTERNATIONAL FEMALE TOP TEN

INTERNATIONAL TOP FEMALE TEN

Maverick: It's classified. I could tell you, but then I'd have to kill you.

1. ROXETTE

Most people think that Roxette is the stunning blonde Swedish temptress that sings 'The Look', 'Listen to Your Heart' and 'It Must Have Been Love', however Roxette is the band's name. The ride's name is Marie Fredriksson (the other bloke in the band is a guy called Per Gessle).

2. BO DEREK

Bo was nominated for a Golden Raspberry in the category of 'Worst Actress of the Century' in the year 2000. It doesn't matter though; Bo was and still is stunning. She is currently dating Carrie's Aidan (John Corbett) from *Sex and the City* and has appeared in lots of editions of *Playboy* dating back to the mid-eighties, if you wish to have a google.

3. JULIA ROBERTS

78% of Irish '80s boys surveyed said that Julia had the best smile of the '80s.

4. KYLIE MINOGUE

39% of single Irish '80s girls worry that if Kylie cannot find love, how in the name of George Clooney are they meant to find someone?

5. KELLY KAPLOWSKI

Most '80s girls were unbelievably jealous of Kelly (Tiffani Thiessen) from *Saved by the Bell* as she had Zack and Slater fighting over her.

6. DENISE FROM THE COSBY SHOW

Denise (Lisa Bonet) has an '80s Kid with Lenny Kravitz.

7. CADBURY'S CARAMEL BUNNY

In a survey of Irish '80s Kids, the Caramel Bunny was voted the sexiest cartoon character of all time, surprisingly ahead of Jessica Rabbit, Betty Boop, Jasmine from *Aladdin* and April O'Neill.

8. KELLY MCGILLIS

(CHARLIE IN *TOP GUN*)
We didn't really have a clue what they were on about, but *Top Gun* was the coolest film of the '80s and Kelly was dead sexy.

Charlie: Excuse me, Lieutenant. Is there something wrong?

Maverick: Yes ma'am, the data on the MiG is inaccurate.

Charlie: How's that, Lieutenant?

Maverick: Well, I just happened to see a MiG 28 do a...

Goose: We!

*Maverick: Uh, sorry, Goose. *We* happened to see a MiG 28 do a 4g negative dive.*

Charlie: Where did you see this?

Maverick: Uh, that's classified.

Charlie: It's what?

9. PRINCESS DIANA

Diana's cousins include Audrey Hepburn, Humphrey Bogart, Rainier III, Terry Phelan and Derek Davis. Her ancestors included Mary Queen of Scots, Lady Catherine Grey, Mary Boleyn, Robert I (The Bruce), Manuel from *Fawlty Towers* and Anne Frank.

10. JAMIE LEE CURTIS

Contrary to internet rumours, JLC is not a hermaphrodite. She had one of the fittest '80s bodies going!

OTHER SEXY MINXES

KIM CATTRALL

DARYL HANNAH

VANESSA MARCIL

CINDY CRAWFORD

SHANNON DOHERTY

KIM BASINGER

DANA (*STAR TREK*)

BELINDA CARLISLE

BANANARAMA GIRLS

HEATHER LOCKLEAR

WHITNEY HOUSTON

PETER BURNS, DEAD OR ALIVE

MADONNA

SAMANTHA FOX

SHARON STONE

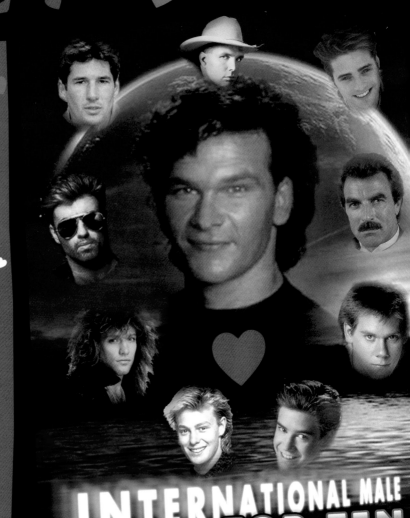

INTERNATIONAL MALE TOP TEN

INTERNATIONAL MALE TOP TEN

1. PATRICK SWAYZE

Swayze's sexiness in both *Dirty Dancing* and *Ghost* were the reasons behind him claiming 41% of the vote for the top International male Sex/Shift, Wear, Score, Meet Symbol. The fact that he is 'brown bread' may also have helped.

2. RICHARD GERE

Richard's middle name is Tiffany. And in the early '90s, it is rumoured that Gere was admitted into the emergency room of a LA hospital with a foreign object lodged in his arse from a solo sex game gone wrong. Gere was alone when he arrived, and an x-ray was taken. The doctors soon discovered that the foreign object was a live gerbil. Gere was then allegedly rushed to surgery, where it took an entire team of surgeons several hours to extract the shaven, lubricated and declawed gerbil 'Tibet'. When the rather invasive procedure was complete, Gere then allegedly paid 'hush money' to the entire surgery and emergency room staff, before allegedly doing the John Wayne walk out of the hospital.

3. GEORGE MICHAEL

George Michael never smiled properly until he got his teeth 'done' in the nineties, due to his teeth looking like a vandalised graveyard.

4. JON BON JOVI

The term 'Bon Jovi' translates as 'happy ending' in Maori.

5. JASON DONOVAN

58% of Irish '80s girls surveyed said they dreamed of finding a man like Scott (Jason) from *Neighbours*.

6. KEVIN BACON

During the creation of the 1998 film *Wilds Things*, Kevin was delighted when he read the script and saw that this was the night where he got to video Neve Campbell and Denise Richards shifting the head off each other in the pool. But when he got to work, the director shot him holding the camera and making ogling and 'turned on' faces without the two rides even being around. He then got sent home as the crew filmed the two girls. Kevin was not happy.

7. TOM SELLECK

Tom received 79% of the vote in a survey of 100 Irish '80s Kids, when asked 'Who had the best 'tache in the '80s?'

8. JASON PRIESTLEY

Jason Priestly (Brandon) was the main man and most girl's fantasy Sex/Shift, Wear, Score, Meet object in 90210. However his rival Brian Austin Green (David) has married and is therefore obviously jaunting Megan Fox. Where did it all go wrong Jason?

9. ZACK MORRIS

Zack (Mark-Paul Gosselaar) dated his three main co-stars, Kelly Kapowski (Tiffani Thiessen), Lisa Marie Turtle (Lark Voorhies) and Jessica 'Jessie' Myrtle Spano (Elizabeth Berkley), during the five years of *Saved By The Bell* – the legend.

10. GARTH BROOKS

Garth Brooks is one of the author's heroes and he is one of the main reasons for the line-dancing phenomenon of the early to mid-nineties throughout Ireland. Most people who voted for Garth as an International Sex/Shift, Wear, Score, Meet Symbol commented that they only did so on the presumption that he had his hat on. They said he went from an 8 to a 3 when he removed his cowboy hat.

OTHER SEXY BEASTS

JOHN CUSACK
MICHAEL BOLTON
TED DANSON
STEVE GUTTENBERG
DAVID HASSELHOFF
CHARLIE SHEEN
MICHAEL DOUGLAS
RICHARD GRIECO
BILLY RAY CYRUS
BRIAN AUSTIN GREEN
BRAD PITT
RICK ASTLEY
COMMANDER RIKER (*STAR TREK*)
JOHN TRAVOLTA
COREY FELDMAN
ROB LOWE
RICHARD DEAN ANDERSON
JOHNNY DEPP
GEORGE CLOONEY
BROS
JOHN CLAUDE VAN DAMME
STEVEN SEAGAL
A-HA SINGER, MORTEN HARKET
SHAKIN' STEVENS

CHAPTER 9

THE BOOKS + MAGAZINES

In a survey of 100 Irish '80s Kids, 78% read books regularly as children. Now compare this with a survey of kids born after the year 1991, in which it was found that only 43% of boys and girls read on a regular basis. Doesn't really bode well for the potential sales figures for The '90s Kid in the coming years!

The lads will remember the Hardy Boys (try reading them now, the little racists!), Roy of the Rovers, and of course the football sticker albums – the bane of parents' lives across the country. The '80s girls will remember reading Malory Towers, which taught them how to be ladies, and Just Seventeen, which taught them how not to be.

So if you want to find out whether Ann and Barry, the '80s answer to Ross and Rachel, made it after all, read on.

SCHOOL ♥

We would read Ann and Barry and could not wait to move on to the next reader to see what

those crazy cats would get up to!! Happy Days was the next book, followed by Lots of Fun and then Fun on the Farm. Taking turns to read in class was a nightmare and I would try to take strategic trips to the loo to avoid it.

Pat & Ann to Ann & Barry to Tara & Ben

The first books that most of us read were our readers in junior infants. Some of you might remember Pat and Ann, then it moved on to Ann and Barry and around 1990 it changed to Tara and Ben. The books got progressively less sexist over the years due to feminist complaints, and even started to become sexist towards men!

Pat and Ann: 'Pat is playing with his truck and Ann is helping Mammy with the washing.' Ann and Barry: 'Barry is helping Daddy in the Garden and Ann is helping Mammy in the kitchen.' Tara and Ben: 'Ben is helping Daddy with dinner and Tara is having a whiskey and a cigar with Mammy.'

LEISURE READING
My Book Review

ENID BLYTON

Anything by Enid Blyton – even though she died in 1968, her stories were a big part of my childhood in the '80s and '90s.

100 IRISH '80S BOYS AND GIRLS WERE ASKED TO CHOOSE THEIR FAVOURITE FAMOUS FIVE CHARACTER ... RESULT: TIMMY 29%, JULIAN 22%, GEORGE 19%, DICK 18% AND ANNE 12%.

MALORY TOWERS

I loved Malory Towers. You can keep your Hogwarts and Gryffindor, I would have liked to have gone to Malory Towers and hung with Darrell Rivers and the North Tower posse. Set in a boarding school for girls in Cornwall, the books follow Darrell and Co. through their six years of secondary school. A whole lot of mild-mannered action takes place and the girls try not to upset the strict Miss Potts and the Matron, who was a right wagon.

GIRLS WHO ATTEND 'FEMALE ONLY' BOARDING SCHOOLS ARE SEVEN TIMES MORE LIKELY TO MAKE BETTER HOUSEWIVES THAN GIRLS WHO ATTEND NORMAL SECONDARY SCHOOLS.

THE POOR CHILD'S GUIDE

THE ORIGINAL VERISON	→	THE POOR MAN'S VERISON
Famous Five	→	Secret Seven
Malory Towers	→	The Girls of St Clare's
Lionel Ritchie	→	Billy Ocean

THE MAGIC FARAWAY TREE

Another Blyton classic.

3% OF '80S KIDS CLAIM TO HAVE SEEN THE MAGIC FARAWAY TREE WHEN UNDER THE INFLUENCE OF ALCOHOL, DRUGS AND/OR CAVAN COLA.

BUZZLESS BEER

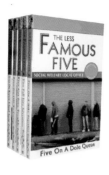

FAMOUS FIVE

I had the 21 Famous Five books and they were my bible growing up. On my bucket list is a trip to Cornwall where I would hunt gold ingots by day and by night, I would drink lashings of ginger beer and eat beef tongue for supper before turning into my bed of bracken (heather) … Five Go to Smuggler's Top was my favourite book. Most of Blyton's books were critically hammered for being sexist and not very PC. One of my memories is when George's mother is in hospital. An aunt is then sent to come and look after the kids, even though Uncle Quentin has two perfectly functioning arms and legs! The aunt is a bit of a fecker and doesn't feed the gang correctly, according to Julian (I wanted to be Julian – as he was on the cusp of adulthood and I wanted the respect and responsibility he got from the grown ups!), so the Five pack up the bags and baggage and head for George's Kirrin Island in the bay.

28% OF IRISH '80S KIDS WHO READ THE FAMOUS FIVE THOUGHT THAT THE GANG WERE DRINKING ALCOHOL WHEN THEY CONTINUOUSLY REFERRED TO THE COPIOUS AMOUNTS OF GINGER ALE AND GINGER BEER IN THE BOOKS.

ROALD DAHL ☾

Roald Dahl's books were probably a lot of people's favourites and the illustrations by Quentin Blake were brilliant. There are so many classics to choose from and many have been turned into movies: Charlie and the Chocolate Factory, Charlie and the Great Glass Elevator, Danny the Champion of the World, Fantastic Mr Fox, James and the Giant Peach, Matilda, The BFG, The Twits and The Witches.

THE BOOK AND FILM THE WITCHES SCARED THE LIVING SHITE OUT OF 79% OF '80S KIDS.

THE HARDY BOYS

The Hardy Boys were massive. The cousins and myself would buy the different ones and swap with each other when we finished them. Frank and Joe Hardy were who we all aspired to be; they were kind of like a pair of young MacGyvers.

A FEW OF THE EARLY EDITIONS OF THE HARDY BOYS WERE HEAVILY CRITICISED, AS AFRICAN AMERICANS WERE THE TARGETS OF MUCH RACISM, AND WERE OPENLY DEPICTED AS UNINTELLIGENT, LAZY, AND SUPERSTITIOUS.

NICE & HARDY

NANCY DREW

The big question for me was which of The Hardy Boys was going to snare Nancy Drew. They appeared a number of times in each other's books and in a number of TV shows. When they got together, you could cut the sexual tension with a knife. My money was on a Joe Hardy, he seemed so dreamy.

☾

OUR SURVEY SAYS...

Character	%
CHARLIE BUCKET	4%
AUGUSTUS GLOOP	12%
VIOLET BEAUREGARDE	15%
MIKE TEAVEE	22%
VERUCA SALT	47%

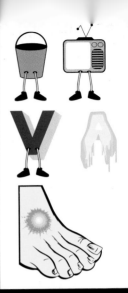

The survey results of 100 Irish '80s kids when asked 'which Charlie and the Chocolate Factory character they would most like to shoot repeatedly with a spud gun from a foot away?'

THE BABY-SITTERS CLUB

A bunch of best friends living in Stoneybrook, Connecticut. They start a business called The Baby-sitters Club, and spend their evenings minding the kids of the neighbourhood for money. There was Kristy Thomas, Mary Anne Spier, Claudia Kishi, and Stacey McGill, all 13, and they had great craic. Myself and the girls in my estate started a babysitters club, but we were too selfish to throw money into a kitty, except when we wanted to buy Hooch for the Friday night on the local green where we went for drunken shifting sessions.

♥

POINT HORROR

I heard these books have been reworked in recent times but the ones of the late '80s were pretty great. R.L. Stine of Goosebumps fame wrote this series and it included some pretty crap titles like Beach Party, The Boyfriend and The Babysitter. They were always based around young teenagers who suffered some pretty horrific, weird and decidedly creepy injuries and deaths. The baddy was usually someone who knew the gang and it would have you guessing until the end. The most important part for me was that sometimes the books had a bit of dirt and raunchiness. You would have one or two of the gang shifting in the forest or shifting at the back of a house when they were meant to be babysitting, when all of a sudden a bad thing would happen...

3

TOP TIPS

INVEST IN A LITTLE BOTTLE OF NIGHT NURSE, PHENERGAN OR JAMESON (NAGGIN) IF YOU ARE BABYSITTING A YOUNG CHILD. IF HE/SHE WILL NOT GO TO SLEEP AND YOU ARE TRYING TO SHIFT YOUR BOYFRIEND ON THE SOFA AFTER WATCHING THE END OF ARMAGEDDON WHERE BRUCIE SACRIFICES HIMSELF FOR THE FUTURE HAPPINESS OF HIS DAUGHTER, EVEN THOUGH AFFLECK GOT THE SHORT STRAW (THIRD FILM I HAVE CRIED AT AFTER BEACHES AND ALL DOGS GO TO HEAVEN), GO UPSTAIRS AND DIP THEIR SOOTHER INTO ONE OF THE AFOREMENTIONED LIQUIDS AND YOU WILL BE BACK AT FIRST BASE IN NO TIME AT ALL.

WIM KIEFT

FOOTBALL STICKER ALBUMS

I did not read books growing up, unless you count that time that the mother signed me over to priests for a two-week retreat in a monastery for bold boys. They had me reading some pretty far-fetched fiction about some fella with a beard feeding thousands with a few bits of sliced pan and fish fingers or something. Anyway, I was a big football fan and I loved 'collecting' the stickers for the Euro '88 and Italia '90 Panini sticker albums. Kids would bring the stickers in to school for swapsies and I would take them as I ruled the playground. Gary Keegan from my class would get a purple snack everyday with his sandwiches, and for a good 4 years from 2nd to 6th class, that was my snack.

EURO '88 WAS COMPLETED WITHOUT A SINGLE PLAYER BEING SENT OFF, ANY KNOCKOUT MATCHES GOING INTO EXTRA TIME OR PENALTIES AND HAVING AT LEAST ONE GOAL SCORED IN EVERY MATCH.

FACT

EURO 88
EUROPEAN CHAMPIONSHIP STICKER ALBUM

SOUTH

CHA BUM KUN

FECK SCHILLACI

SHOT! KIDNAPPED! BLOWN UP! HELICOPTER CRASH! AMPUTEE!

ROY OF THE ROVERS

The hero. This comic was the 'Dream Team' of its time ... Roy was brilliant at football, he had lots of money, he could have any woman he wanted yet married the club secretary, and he was shot, and kidnapped at least five times. His team bus was blown up resulting in the death of eight teammates (he escaped with a dislocated shoulder) and was in a helicopter crash that resulted in the amputation of his foot!!

I was a Match man from the beginning. There were interviews, funny stories, great wall posters, transfer gossip, quizzes and a weekly round-up of results and tables. At the start of each season, you would get a free table tracker with little cardboard team names for each of the four English divisions, which you hung on your bedroom wall and swore you would update every week. Also during the summer, you would get a free Merlin FA Premier League sticker album with an edition of Match. The poor parents, grandparents, aunts and uncles would be hit for a couple of packets of stickers a week. The packets were definitely rigged. Every single season, most people were left with 7 or 8 swaps of superstars like Jason Dodd, Gary Flitcroft and Ian Woan.

SHOOT CLOSED ITS DOORS FOR THE FINAL TIME IN 2008.

CUT OUT WARDROBE ♥

Bunty was my favourite magazine and contained lots of comic strips and other girly stories. Most editions contained a story about 3 or 4 girls with the same name like 'The Three Alices' or 'The Four Fionas' and then detailed the adventures that they would get up to. It would get delivered to the local newsagent on a Saturday. I would torment the Mam and drag her out of bed at 10am every week to get it, much to my father's annoyance as he liked to 'lie-on' every weekend with Mammy.

FACT

TIN TIN IS NOT GAY AND SNOWY IS NOT A GAY DOG, CONTRARY TO MOST PEOPLE'S BELIEF.

FACT

29% OF IRISH '80S KIDS PARENTS WOULD HAVE THEIR BEDROOM LOCKED AT A CERTAIN TIME MOST SATURDAY AND/OR SUNDAY MORNINGS, FOR WHATEVER REASON.

FACT

The Beano is probably the more famous of the two major rivals. The Dandy has Desperate Dan and Bananaman, who are two of my favourite comic characters of all time.

Whereas The Beano has a host of famous and iconic characters such as Roger the Dodger, Minnie the Minx, The Bash Street Kids, Calamity James, Ivy the Terrible, Billy Whizz and the brilliant Dennis the Menace (who John Paul obviously models himself on!).

In 2007, The Dandy was disgracefully rebranded Dandy Xtreme and it was the first time a Dandy character did not appear on the cover – Bart Simpson did. In 2010, it changed back to The Dandy.

THE DANDY VS THE BEANO

THE BEANO COMIC TAKES ITS NAME FROM THE ENGLISH WORD 'BEANO', WHICH CAN BE LOOSELY INTERPRETED AS A GOOD TIME.

FACT

ESPECIALLY FOR YOU

Just Seventeen magazine was my fortnightly guidebook. It was full of fashion, real stories, problem pages and teen advice that was hugely beneficial to me in my adult life. Things like: always be wary of all men, never trust a man who tries a chat-up line and always wear nice knickers in case you are knocked down and the doctor who saves you takes a shine to you. J-17's last edition was in 2004.

♥

TOUCH ME

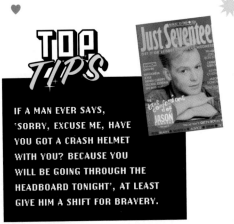

TOP TIPS

IF A MAN EVER SAYS, 'SORRY, EXCUSE ME, HAVE YOU GOT A CRASH HELMET WITH YOU? BECAUSE YOU WILL BE GOING THROUGH THE HEADBOARD TONIGHT', AT LEAST GIVE HIM A SHIFT FOR BRAVERY.

Smash Hits Magazine was feckin' huge. It was the main mag for most girls between the ages of 12 to 16 and featured all the pop stars of the day. It even had the lyrics to all the chart hits and came out every second Thursday. It was a must-buy if only for the amazing posters of Take That, Bros, New Kids on the Block, etc. It survived until 2006, but was never better than in its '80s heyday. ♥

How My Body Works was a weekly series of books which was available in the shops. Every book came with a body part and once the collection was complete, you had a plastic man with all the main body parts inside. The books were great and they were turned into a TV series called 'Once Upon a Time – Life' that was shown on Saturdays. This series was great and the manager of the brain was a little white-bearded man called Maestro. The episode called the 'Chain of Life' was my favourite as I felt bold watching it, even though it was the most mild-mannered birds and bees lesson ever!

NOW LOOK INTO MY EYE

Magic Eye Patterns was a booklet full of weird-looking patterns similar to what you would see if you looked through a kaleidoscope or if you looked at your father's or uncle's horrible '80s and '90s dog-tooth check blazers for too long. Supposedly, if you looked at the static-on-TV-like patterns the correct way, you were meant to see a 3D image, however most people lied and looked at the page that told you what you should be seeing! ♥

CHAPTER 10

THE HAIRCUTS

Have a look at these haircuts. I bet you'll find at least three haircuts that you 'rocked' in the '80s. Most were appalling, in a wonderful way, and the fact that none of these styles have really made into the twenty-first century is testament to just how brilliantly bad they really were. The hair was big, it was long, it was accessorised, crimped, permed, stepped and generally styled to within an inch of its life. NOTHING was out of the question (apart from being near open flames).

TEMPORARY HAIR DYE   HINT OF A TINT

CLAIROL GLINTS   SUN-IN

THE STEP

PONY-TAILS AND RAT TAILS FOR MEN

HAIR CRIMPING

BUSINESS AT THE FRONT

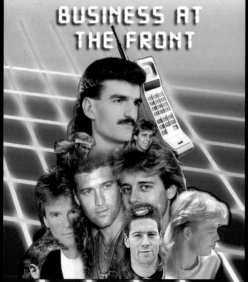

PARTY IN THE BACK !!!

THE CURTAINS

THE MULLET

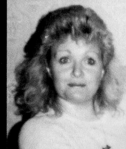

138

FLATTOP

THE BOWL
THE MOTHERCUT
AUNTIECUT

PIGTAILS

SIDE
PONYTAIL

FLOCK OF
SEAGULLS

THE
MOTHERCUT

PUNKY
Brewster
Season One

Hair

BACK COMBING
AND GENERALLY
JUST BIG HAIR

139

THE CURTAINS

Probably more of a '90s cut, but I admit to having The Curtains with an undercut. I had what I considered to be a cute floppy-haired style with a central parting and two flops of hair down each side. When I was playing football or generally just moving about, the hair would annoy the hell out of me and kept getting in the way of my eyes. The girls loved me when the Backstreet Boys came on the scene in the mid-'90s though – they said I was like a young and skinny Nick Carter.

THE LADS WITH THE CURTAINS HAIRCUT ALWAYS HAD THE MOST LUCK WITH THE WOMEN IN IBIZA UNCOVERED. *FACT*

THE STEP

I had The Step, as did most lads around my way. It was a haircut that was not blended. It looked like you had one layer, and then another layer and the non-blending looked like distinct lines in the head .... Most lads went for the double Step, the mad boyos went for the treble Step and I had five Steps. A dwarf could have used the back of my head to get in a window.

29% OF IRISH '80S BOYS SURVEYED HAD A STEP AT SOME STAGE IN THE '80S AND/OR '90S. *FACT*

THE MULLET

Pretty much everyone (if you were a someone!) had a mullet in the '80s. Some of the most notable mullets of the time were Pat Sharp, Billy Ray Cyrus, Michael Bolton, Bono, Bon Jovi, Chris Waddle, Glen Hoddle and Jason Donovan. It is often referred to as the 'Business at the front, partaaaaaaaay in the back!' haircut. However, in my humble opinion, it is almost as shocking in the front.

SOME LADIES EVEN EXPERIMENTED WITH THE MULLET. *FACT*

FLATTOP

I had one of these too. The Flattop was fairly big in the '80s and action films like Top Gun definitely aided in its popularity. Think Ivan 'If he dies he dies' Drago, from Rocky IV's hairstyle. I kind of looked like him with my blond hair in a short back 'n' sides with a square Flattop, except that I had as high a forehead as Uncle Fester.

PONYTAILS AND RAT TAILS FOR MEN

A fair few of the aul' lads around my way would have had little crappy pony or rat tails. Most were drug dealers, karaoke performers, washing machine repairmen and wannabe pornstars.

FACT

DARREN DAY 33%, ASHLEY COLE 33% AND RYAN GIGGS 33% WERE THE SURVEY RESULTS OF THREE IRISH '80S GIRLS WHEN ASKED WHO HAD THE BEST EVER RAT TAIL IN THE HISTORY OF THE UNIVERSE.

THE BOWL

THE MOTHERCUT

THE AUNTIECUT

Getting the steps in the hair was a once-a-year treat for me when the mother got her bonus for having another illegitimate child in the Rotunda. The usual job on my hair was done on a trip down to the auntie's for a haircut by big black-handled scissors and a bowl. My fringe always bleedin' ended up crooked too.

TEMPORARY HAIR DYE

CLAIROL GLINTS

HINT OF A TINT

SUN-IN

Both boys and girls experimented with all of these. For some reason a gang of lads around my neighbourhood decided to dye their hair plum for a summer. They were not even middle-class Goths rebelling against their slightly above average upbringing, they were normal lads who enjoyed football, Devils Bit and shifting. Strange. All the girls would have tried Sun-In or lemon juice during the various summers with varying degrees of success.

- - - - - - - -

HAIR CRIMPING

Hair crimping was huge. I did not leave the house for 2 years without the hair crimped. The influence of Cyndi Lauper and Madonna meant that you were a loser if you were not crimped. Before my best friend and I got a Babyliss crimper off Santa one year (it was wrecked and full of burnt hairspray after a month from overuse), we would spend hours upon hours one evening a week plaiting each other's hair in the tiniest of plaits before wetting it and going to bed. We would then wake up and rush over to one of our houses and unravel the hundred or so plaits to reveal extra frizzy crimped hair.

TOP TIPS

NEVER ALLOW YOUR AUNT, WHO HAS A NEARLY PERMANENT TREMOR FROM WITHDRAWALS OF CHARDONNAY, TO CUT YOUR FRINGE UNTIL SHE HAS HAD A FEW GLASSES OF WINE THAT DAY.

SIDE PONYTAIL

For another few years in the '80s I rocked the Side Ponytail. I would draw all my flowing locks to one side and pile it as high on my head as I could get it. I would then tie it up in one of my illuminous hair bands and stand and sing into my hairbrush in front of the mirror, thinking I was Tiffany.

- - - - - - - -

PIGTAILS

I used to love Punky Brewster and her pigtails. I would split my hair perfectly evenly down the middle and gather it into a ponytail on each side of my head to copy her.

PIPPI LONGSTOCKING KILLED PUNKY BREWSTER BY STRANGULATION DURING A CELEBRITY DEATHMATCH ENCOUNTER.

- - - - - - - - FACT

BACK COMBING AND GENERALLY JUST BIG HAIR

The aim was to make our hair as big, tall and bold as possible. The girls and myself would hang each other upside down over the bed to blow dry the hair with tonnes of product with the aim of getting as much volume in the hair as possible. The overarching objective was for the hair to defy gravity.

FACT

THE BACKCOMBING BRIGADE IS BACK IN FORCE. THESE EXTRAORDINARY 15-TO-18-YEAR-OLD SPECIMENS CAN BE FOUND IN THE CROWDED SUBURBAN BADLANDS OF DUBLIN'S DUNDRUM SHOPPING CENTRE, DRESSED IN OVERSIZE ABERCROMBIE AND HOLLISTER HOODIES (THAT THEIR OLDER BROTHER/SISTER/ BOYFRIEND BROUGHT HOME FROM THEIR MENTALLY SORDID J1 TO SAN DIEGO THE PREVIOUS YEAR) AND O'NEILLS OR CANTERBURY TRACKIE BOTTOMS, COUPLED WITH TOP-OF-THE-RANGE UGGS. AROUND 12PM ON ANY DAY OF THE SUMMER HOLIDAYS, THEY CAN BE OBSERVED SUCKLING ON MOCHA COKA FRAPULORANGINA-PACINOS AND SUSHI BAGELS (AS SANDWICHES ARE SOOOOOOOOO NORTHSIDE) BEFORE CHEWING ON NICORETTE GUM AS THEY SHOOT THE BREEZE ABOUT HOW DADDY IS SUCH A 'LEDGE' AS HE INCREASED THEIR WEEKLY ALLOWANCE TO 400 EUROS AND OPENED A TAB IN BT2.

- - - - - - - - - ✂

FLOCK OF SEAGULLS

A flock of seagulls were an average enough band from Liverpool. They had a few half-decent hits in the '80s however they are probably best known for the lead singer Mike Score's wonderfully horrific haircut, the 'The Flock of Seagulls'.

Accessories

TIFFANY
KYLIE
CYNDI
CHERI
KERRI
FUDGER

HAIRBANDS WITH YOUR NAME ON IT

BANANA CLIPS

SCRUNCHIES FACT

SCRUNCHIES ARE NOW GENERALLY WORN IN COMBINATION WITH PYJAMAS BY GIRLS IN VARIOUS URBAN CENTRES AROUND THE COUNTRY AS THEY GO ABOUT THEIR DAILY BUSINESS OF SHOPPING AND CHATTING UP LADS WHO GO AROUND WITH THEIR HANDS IN THEIR JOCKS.

CLAIROL BENDERS

CLAIROL BENDERS SOUNDS LIKE A HALF-DECENT SLAG. FACT

CHAPTER 11

THE CLOTHES + ACCESSORIES

'80s clobber was a colourful crossover of men's and women's fashions: loose-fitting, tight-fitting, nothing-in-between, heavily accessorised, androgynous shite. It was superb. Looks were inspired by the media; by TV, movies, music and porn stars, it would seem. Fabrics were gaudy, synthetic and highly flammable, and the rule for accessories was, 'more is more'. Snazzy Bermuda shorts with white socks and black shoes? Why not! Bomber jackets over tie-dye jumpers? Of course! Cycling shorts and bumbags? Hell yes. Your Dad would go around in a Don Johnson Miami Vice pastel suit; your Mam headed off to bingo dressed like Pauline Fowler in a handmade jumper, pedal-pushers and a reversible anorak; your sister fancied herself in her Jennifer Beals-style leotards, leg warmers and oversized sweatshirts, and you went on your merry way to school with light-up runners, knowing that they would get stamped on and wrecked within 30 seconds. Those were the days.

FULL BODY

DRESSING UP IN ANY COSTUME

When we were growing up, our daily attire consisted of a variety of character costumes. One day I would be Batman, Superman the next and the girls in the neighbourhood would wear their communion dresses out on the road (when their Mammys were out for the day) pretending to be Cinderella, some princess or Daniel O'Donnell when he is at home.

SHELL SUITS/ FLECKY TRACKSUITS

I used to float around my estate in my shell suit. I had a savage umbro one. The only downside with wearing this was when I dropped ash from my normal and funny cigarettes. It would leave horrible-looking burn marks.

THE AUTHOR HAD A GREEN AND WHITE SHELL SUIT AND WORE IT TO PRIMARY SCHOOL FOR THE HALLOWEEN FANCY DRESS DAY IN 1990. HE WALKED AROUND ON HIS TIPTOES FOR THE WHOLE DAY AND CLAIMED TO BE NIALL QUINN. HIS TEACHER DID NOT GET IT AND WOULD NOT LET HIM ENTER THE COMPETITION FOR £1. HE WAS NOT FECKIN' HAPPY.

HAND-ME-DOWNS FROM THE BROTHERS, SISTERS & COUSINS

A big black plastic sack of clothes would arrive from the aunt, filled with the older cousins' unwanted clothes, a couple of times a year. I can remember the excitement as you scrummaged for jumpers, shirts, jeans and shoes. You would take a few nice little numbers before the mother stepped in and started to pick clothes for you. Of course the mother would pick the naffest gear that you would not even force the little shit of a cousin that no one really liked to wear. She was more label conscious than you, and no matter how small or big the item of clobber was, once it was Benetton, fake Armani, etc., you would be wearing it to mass that Sunday.

TOP HALF CLOBBER

GERMAN ARMY JACKETS AND SHIRTS

I never wore this range myself, but I always wondered what the fascination was. I was still quite young in the early '90s when a lot of the older lads started wearing these jackets in khaki green or grey that had a little German flag on the upper arm. I just did not get it and I still don't. These days you still see the odd greasy, spotty, long-haired male teenager sporting the old West German coat, but thankfully, these sightings are few and far between.

BENETTON SWEATSHIRTS

These were so hot in the late '80s and early '90s. I had three Benetton jumpers in three lovely pastel colours – sky blue, yellow and green. I just refused to wear anything else for about a year. If the family were going for a 'fancy' meal, I would just throw a black polo neck on underneath and that instantly turned me into a classy chick, or so I thought.

BENETTON'S AD FROM THE EARLY '90S FEATURING A NEWBORN BABY GIRL COVERED IN BLOOD WITH ITS UMBILICAL CORD STILL ATTACHED IS ONE OF THE MOST CONTROVERSIAL ADVERTISEMENTS OF ALL TIME.

DENIM JACKETS

The denim jacket has been around for many decades but probably peaked in popularity in the '80s. I wore mine with everything: dresses, skirts, jeans, trousers and even with just a pair of knickers to impress this American guy who I was seeing, who looked a bit like Garth Brooks. I had a few normal classic-cut jackets, including one with faux sheepskin lining, along with a cropped version that was stone and acid-washed. My major turn off in men is matching or mismatching denim jeans and jacket combo. There are only two men that can pull that off and their names are Jean Claude Van Damme and Larry Mullen Jr.

FACT

HYPERCOLOUR AND SCRATCH 'N' SNIFF T-SHIRTS

I thought that these t-shirts were the best invention ever and that they would take over from normal Ts. I had a little blue number and when I started sweating it would turn orange. I remember when I first got it, I went straight for the mother's hairdryer to see if it worked.

Scratch 'n' Sniff t-shirts were the business. I thought that this was the way forward and that normal t-shirts would be phased out for being boring – they smelled of nothing!! Scratch 'n' Sniffs came in Chocolate, Cheese, Strawberry, Cherry, Fart, Banana, Mint, Bugglegum and lots more flavours.

♥

FACT

AFTER SIX WASHES THE SCRATCH 'N' SNIFF AROMA WOULD WEAR OFF, BUT WHY IN THE NAME OF MACGYVER WOULD ANYONE WANT TO WALK AROUND SMELLING OF CHEESE ANYWAY?

IF THE HYPERCOLOUR COMES BACK 'IN' TO FASHION, DO NOT LET YOUR SONS OR DAUGHTERS WEAR IT TO SCHOOL. MY MEMORIES ARE OF PEOPLE COMING UP TO ME IN MY HYPERCOLOUR AND BREATHING ON ME, TWISTING THE SHIRT, THROWING WATER (PLUS OTHER LIQUIDS THAT I WON'T GET IN TO) AND MAULING ME WITH THEIR HANDS IN ORDER TO LEAVE HANDPRINTS. IT REALLY PROVIDED A FANTASTIC OPPORTUNITY TO MOLEST A CLASSMATE.

TOP TIPS

ANYTHING WITH POLKA

Polka Dots have been around for a long time but were another big fad in the late '80s. It was not long after this that the cult classic and most horny male teenagers favourite music video 'Itsy Bitsy Teeny Weeny Yellow Polka Dot Bikini' by Bombalurina came out in 1990.

TIMMY MALLET OF WACADAY FAME WAS THE SINGER IN BOMBALURINA AND ONE OF THE HOTTIES FROM THE VIDEO WAS DAWN ANDREWS (NOW DAWN BARLOW AFTER MARRYING GARY BARLOW).

FACT

MALLETT'S MA

LOWER HALF CLOBBER

REALLY REALLY RIPPED AND BLEACHED JEANS

PATCHING UP THE KNEES ON YOUR JEANS

I was not a huge fan of the rips. I had my joe bloggs stonewash jeans with two patches from all the time I spent on my knees .... playing marbles, doing dips, bashing the letter and begging the mother not to hit me after she came in from the pub.

The more frayed and wrecked the better they were. The non-uniform days in school were great. I remember the school hottie, Sean Bonner, from a few years ahead, came in with extreme rips in his ultra 'distressed' jeans. There were so many holes that you could see his hairy legs and the bottom of his arse. He got sent home but I could see that a few of the younger female teachers did not agree with the principal's decision.

SPANDEX AND CYCLE SHORTS

Not a very flattering look for a lot of females and a few males around my way. Spandex and ridiculously tight leggings were all the rage in the '80s. It was probably the influence of the Jane Fonda Workout videos for the elder ladies, Fame/ Flashdance for the younger girls and Mr Motivator's and Linford Christie's lunchboxes for the pervy ones.

FOOT WEAR

CLARKS MAGIC STEPS

I had three different pairs! They were the best shoes for girls, and everyone wanted them. Magic Steps had a gold key and a jewel in the sole of the shoe that you could uncover with the magical key!

IN A SURVEY OF ONE HUNDRED FEMALE IRISH '80S KIDS, 78% SAID THAT THEY WOULD WEAR A PAIR OF MAGIC STEPS IF THEY WERE RE-RELEASED IN ADULT SIZES.

DOC MARTENS

I got a new pair of Docs every two years throughout primary and secondary school. They were always bought two sizes too big for me so I that could 'grow into them', which meant that I had to wear two pairs of thick socks for that first year.

I had a pair in 'cherry red' and they were either eight or ten hole (eyelets either side of the boot), I can't remember. Most people wore them with coloured laces and I would rotate between yellow and black each week.

DR MARTEN'S WERE THE FAVOURED BOOTS OF THE SKINHEAD MOVEMENT AND MR MARTEN WAS NO DOCTOR.

REEBOK AIR PUMPS VS AIR MAX

Reebok Pumps were the bee's knees. In keeping with the fascination with all things basketball and Michael Jordan in the lates '80s, the Reebok Pumps versus Nike Air Max battle began. The pumps took the lead when they were released and we all wanted that orange basketball-shaped pump on the tongue that would inflate the internal mechanism, causing your runners to suddenly feel too small for you! Air Max really took over in the early '90s and was the only runner to be seen in at the teenage discos. A bright new pair of Air Max nearly guaranteed you a few shifts.

FACT

IN BRIGHTON, BOSTON IN 1989, A RIGHT REEBOK PUMP MALFUNCTIONED CAUSING AN ANTHONY O'SHEA TO GO FROM A UK SIZE 11 TO A SIZE 5. HIS WIFE WAS SOON DEEPLY SEXUALLY FRUSTRATED AND LEFT HIM FOR ANOTHER MAN WHO WAS A SOLID SIZE 9.

LA GEAR

AND OTHER RUNNERS WITH LIGHTS ON THEM AND MULTICOLOURED LACES

Runners that light up and flash when a child's foot touches the ground are still very popular with kids today. They first came on the scene in the '80s. I had a pretty cool black pair of LA Lights that really stood out when we were playing late night Tip the Can on the road, unfortunately.

BONO'S FAVOURITE

PLATFORM SHOES

FOR THAT EXTRA EDGE

Platforms were more of a '70s thing, but a good friend of mine wore them from the early '90s to the mid-noughties, until we sat him down for a wee chat. We were away on a trip and most of the lads were all dolled up for the night in the best of 'clobber'. Our friend steps out of the room in a nice shirt, decent jeans and a pair of feckin' platforms. Needless to say he was ridiculed and abused until he went back to the room to change into a pair of normal shoes.

They are a real favourite of Bono and other diminutive men, but to potential naked lie-down cuddle prospects, they shout 'I have a complex RE my height.' I do feel for my little friend who stares into the mirror most days and sighs 'I have the looks, if only I had the height'. His shoes remained in the hotel room bin when we left a few days later.

ACCESSORIES

MIKASA GLOVES

You may think it is strange to include perceived 'football' gloves in the clothes + accessories chapter, however a pair of Mikasa's were far more than Goalie/GAA gloves. They were the ultimate multi-purpose gloves. If you had a pair of these it turned you into Pagliuca or Jack o'Shea and it enabled you to climb trees, fling dogshite at people, fight, lift bricks, apply fake tan to your aunt (when the black rubber had worn off) and they also acted as hand warmers in the snow.

SHOULDER PADS

The '80s was a time when every woman wanted broader, bigger and sharper shoulders. Power dressing and feminism was rampant in the corporate world in the '80s and masculine styles invaded female fashion. When you think of shoulder pads and power dressing, think of the lovely Dynasty ladies like Joan Collins, think of Melanie Griffiths in Working Girl and think of the three Superman baddies (General Zod, Ursa and Non) clad in black in Superman II. one stage in the mid-eighties, practically every item of clothing for ladies came with its own set of shoulder pads. If that was not enough, separate pads were sold with velcro so you could stack them up for even higher and sharper shoulders.

SLAP BRACELETS OR WRAPS

My arms were full of these. Slap Bracelets were brightly coloured material over this plastic strip that you slapped really hard on your wrist and it coiled around tightly. They were banned from my school pretty quickly.

A GOOD WAY TO HURT YOUNGER KIDS IN SCHOOL WAS TO GET A COLOURFUL 12-INCH RULER AND APPROACH LET'S SAY A SENIOR INFANT. ASK THE KID IF THEY WANT A FREE SLAP BRACELET AND WHEN THEY INEVITABLY SAY YES, ASK THEM TO HOLD OUT THEIR ARM. SLAP THEM AS HARD AS YOU CAN WITH THE RULER AND WATCH THEIR LITTLE FACE TURN ALL SAD WHEN THEY REALISE THEIR NAIVETY. **TOP TIPS**

SWATCH WATCHES

The only watch to have in the '80s was a Swatch. A few of the fads included wearing two Swatches, using a Swatch as a ponytail band and having lots of different Swatch guards to change it up a little every single day.

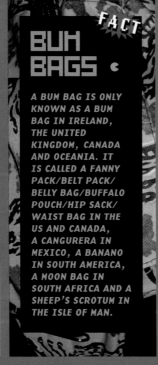

BUM BAGS

FACT

A BUM BAG IS ONLY KNOWN AS A BUM BAG IN IRELAND, THE UNITED KINGDOM, CANADA AND OCEANIA. IT IS CALLED A FANNY PACK/BELT PACK/BELLY BAG/BUFFALO POUCH/HIP SACK/WAIST BAG IN THE US AND CANADA, A CANGURERA IN MEXICO, A BANANO IN SOUTH AMERICA, A MOON BAG IN SOUTH AFRICA AND A SHEEP'S SCROTUM IN THE ISLE OF MAN.

GROLSCH CAPS ON SHOES

A really strange one to end on, that some will remember. I headed down to the pub with Dad on a Sunday in the late '80s, feigned interest in the GAA match on the TV and asked him to have two bottles of Grolsch so I could keep the caps. After he got the second bottle, I ran home and put one cap on each of shoe, attaching them through the shoelace holes. When you walked around they kind of clickity-clacked up and down exactly like the Bros twins – the rides.

CHAPTER 12

THE BIG EVENTS

Hundreds of landmark moments occured in the '80s, from tragic events felt the world over, to Ireland's own little victories. There are the hunger strikes, the Spike Island riots, the Stardust fire, the Hillsborough disaster and the untimely death of John Lennon. The Air India and Lockerbie plane crashes happen, someone shoots Shergar, someone tries to shoot the Pope, no one tries to shoot Thatcher. Ireland takes a battering from Hurricane Charlie and mass emigration, but McGuigan becomes World Champion, Roche wins the Tour De France, Andrew Murray is born, and Day-Lewis plays 'Let Christy take it' Brown. On TV, Charlie and Diana marry, the Bucks Fizz ladies lose their skirts, and Gerry Ryan kills a lamb (or does he?). A statue moves in Ballinspittle and a reasonable individual hijacks an Aer Lingus jet and demands the publication of the Third Secret of Fatima. Charlie 'Charvet' Haughey becomes Taoiseach, women take over the forty foot, and Mary 'Noddy' Robinson is elected Ireland's first female President.

This is the Late Late Toy Show...

This was a massive event every year growing up. It used to be aired in early December (now shown in November) and many kids would hold off from writing their Santa lists until after the show. The anticipation would build all week and you could not wait for 9.30pm that Friday. My usual pre-Toy Show preparation involved being made to have the weekly bath, being put into my He-Man pyjamas and then being given a few Mr Kipling French Fancies iced cakes and a glass of cream soda before Gaybo bounced out in his oversize Christmas jumper!

Roll the VT... Colette, Róisín... whatever your name is.

FACT GAYBO 56%, TUBS 38%, THE PLANK 6% WERE THE SURVEY RESULTS OF 100 IRISH '80S KIDS WHEN ASKED WHO THEY THOUGHT WAS THE BEST TOY SHOW PRESENTER.

Christmas

The biggest annual event for any '80s Kid by far. After I had prepared the carrot for Rudolf and bottle of Guinness for Santa, it was time to hit the leaba on Christmas Eve. No matter what I did (counting sheep, reading until I was tired, thinking about shifting my uncle's new girlfriend on the lips, etc.), I could not go to sleep – the harder I tried, the more awake I felt. Then the worry set in. If I did not get to sleep, Santa could not come into the house and that meant no presents!

Next thing I knew, it was 5am and I was awake. I would leap from the bed and run around the house like a mad man, waking brothers, sisters, Mam and Dad. The parents would make me wait for the whole family to get their dressing gowns and slippers on, and every feckin' year the mother would be scrambling around for batteries for the camera before she would let us into the sitting room to see what Santa had left.

You generally got exactly what you wanted (Big Trak, Atari, BMX, Scalextric, etc.), but it did not really matter, as pretty much all '80s toys were brilliant. The morning was spent playing with all the new toys, watching the Christmas Day edition of The Den and sneaking into the jacks to eat the Curly Wurlys and Crunchies from a carefully opened selection box. Then it was time for Mass, the worst part of the day. You had to leave the toys at home and the Mass was always longer than the usual 40 minutes – nightmare stuff. We then headed to the grandparents for the big Christmas dinner with the extended family and you'd put forward your case that your toys were waaaaaaaay better than your cousins'.

After dinner , where you refused point blank to try a Brussels sprout and then proceeded to eat your own body weight in croquette potatoes with your cousin Alison, more selection boxes would be pocketed. The afternoon involved the kids playing with toys and complaining about the film on the TV that all the oldies were watching being boring and far too long (Gone with the Wind).

After that, the older members of the family collapsed and passed out (I am looking at you here, Uncle Alberto) from the copious amounts of red wine and Satzenbrau for a few hours in front of a blazing fire, before waking up on time for the Christmas special of Only Fools and Horses. Then everyone would drink drive home.

Eurovision 1980 & 1987

Back when the Eurovision was a proper competition and not a feckin' vote for your neighbour contest, Ireland were kind of a big deal (we then took over completely in the '90s). The '80s was a pretty bleak time in Ireland, with high taxes, mass unemployment, and emigration, and it was before the whole nation got behind the Irish football team in '88 and '90, so anything achieved by the country on a European or world scale was considered a huge moment in people's lives. Johnny did us proud by winning with 'What's Another Year' in 1980 and 'Hold Me Now' in 1987 and was an all-round ride! I fancied him, my mother fancied him, my granny fancied him and my cousin Mike did too.

 THE LATE GREAT PATRICK SWAYZE WON A CELEBRITY LOOKALIKE CONTEST IN BIDDY O'DALY'S PUB, NEW YORK, IN MARCH 1983 AS JOHNNY LOGAN.

Who Shot J.R.?

FACT

A MONTHLY SESSION OF TUAM TOWN COUNCIL WAS SUSPENDED TO ALLOW COUNCILLORS A CHANCE TO GET HOME IN TIME TO VIEW THE 'WHO SHOT J.R.' DALLAS EPISODE.

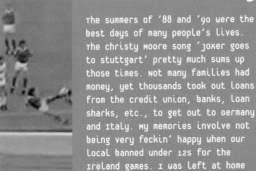

EURO '88 & ITALIA '90

The summers of '88 and '90 were the best days of many people's lives. The Christy Moore song 'Joxer goes to Stuttgart' pretty much sums up those times. Not many families had money, yet thousands took out loans from the credit union, banks, loan sharks, etc., to get out to Germany and Italy. My memories involve not being very feckin' happy when our local banned under 12s for the Ireland games. I was left at home with my granny and a few other cousins, who were girls, to watch the games. They were great times though. After all the games every kid on the road would be diving on the ground pretending to be Packie Bonner, or getting people to throw the ball in to head it between the jumpers for goalposts like Houghton did to the English. A lot of people tried the side shin volley like Ronnie Whelan's famous goal against USSR, but most could not manage to get the right misconnection.

TONY CASCARINO WAS BRUTAL. **FACT**

Knock, Knock... ➘

Listen to the 'Knock Song' by Christy Moore for the full history. Briefly, when the country, and the west of Ireland in particular, was on its knees due to mass unemployment and emigration, a Monsignor James Horan persuaded the government and the European Union to fund an international airport near Kiltimagh (Louis Walsh's home town). Knock International Airport, which was opened in 1986, must be one of the most outrageously located international airports anywhere in the world. It is in a ridiculously rural location, on a bog and close to the top of a large hill. The one surprise is that Ryanair does not fly in to Knock and call it Dublin Knock, just like Paris Beauvais.

IF YOU WANT AN INTERNATIONAL AIRPORT IN A FIELD NEAR YOU: BECOME A PRIEST; MAKE UP A PHONY MIRACLE; MAKE A 10-YEAR PLAN; START RUNNING BINGO TO FUNDRAISE; BUILD AN OLD-PERSON-PLEASING BASILICA; ENCOURAGE THE DEVELOPMENT OF CHIP SHOPS, B&B'S AND RESTAURANTS; PRETEND THE GHOST OF JOE DOLAN APPEARED BESIDE THE FIELD AND SAY THIS ALONE SHOULD ENTITLED YOU TO AN AIRPORT; LOBBY/HARASS TDS AND THREATEN EX-COMMUNICATION; NEED MORE MONEY? - ASK NATO; AND BAM! YOU SHOULD HAVE YOURSELF A FINE LITTLE AIRPORT.

TOP TIPS

FAIRLY SHITTY

LAUNCH OF *FAIR CITY*
once Billy Meehan (my idol) died, I stopped watching it.

FACT BELLA AND RITA DOYLE WERE VOTED THE 2ND MOST ENDEARING IRISH TV COUPLE IN A SURVEY OF 100 IRISH '80S KIDS, JUST BEHIND EAMONN DUNPHY AND JOHNNY GILES.

★ PAT SPILLANE ON INTERNATIONAL SUPERSTARS

At the end of the '70s and beginning of the '80s, we were not used to seeing sporting greats from our little island competing against other 'stars' from around the world. When Pat Spillane got on to International Superstars in the late '70s, it was a massive deal for us. At the start it was fairly inspirational and by the end it was fairly cringeworthy. You see the finals were held in the Bahamas. Pat, the epitome of a fair-haired, milky-skinned Kerryman, wore a t-shirt which made his arms look like slabs of pork due to severe sunburn, just like every stereotypical Irish lad who went on

a Club 18-30 trip to the Med in the '80s. He really struggled with the heat, and after a particularly long and exhausting bike race, he stated that 'the heat is fierce, you'd have to be here to feel it'. It also appeared that he finished last in the swimming event and nearly had to be rescued from the pool. Some well-placed sources have indicated that Pat freely admits to being a below average swimmer, but spotted that there was prize money for the top five in the swimming and only four people had signed up. All he had to do was finish the race and he was, allegedly, in the money!!

LIVE AID & IRELAND'S ANSWER TO IT, 'SELF-AID' – Live Aid was great for heaps of reasons that we all know. Self-Aid in Ireland was great because it was the final performance of the Boomtown Rats. I have tried to explain to a few of the younger generation and a few of the English relations the premise behind Self-Aid, and I always get the same reaction; a laugh and then a 'you are taking the feckin' Michael?' The reason for the concert was to highlight the desperate unemployment problem in Ireland at the time, with nearly 250,000 people unemployed (we probably need to do something right now as we have a hell of a lot more than a quarter of a million unemployed at present – but not another Self-Aid!), which everyone knew and was depressed about already, as you collected your tins of EEC intervention beef at Christmas along with your butter vouchers. Some money was raised in a telethon and some jobs were 'pledged', but it was all very cringey. I do remember it being a very good gig though! You had the likes of Bagatelle, Paul Brady, Chris de Burgh, Cactus World News, De Danann, Rory Gallagher, Christy Moore, Van Morrison, Moving Hearts, The Pogues, Chris Rea, Thin Lizzy (4 months after Phil Lynott died), Those Nervous Animals, U2 and Elvis Costello.

U2 ARE UNDERRATED AND BONO IS A LEGEND.

Image: Phil Coomes

CHERNOBYL NUCLEAR ACCIDENT

A REALLY HORRIBLE DAY IN APRIL 1986. CHERNOBYL IS REGARDED AS THE WORST NUCLEAR POWER PLANT ACCIDENT EVER AND ALL OF IRELAND'S THOUGHTS AND PRAYERS WERE WITH THE POOR PEOPLE OF THE REGION DURING THAT TIME AND IN THE INTERVENING YEARS. I WAS A YOUNG KID WHEN THIS HAPPENED THOUGH AND ONE OF MY LASTING MEMORIES GROWING UP WAS WHEN I EARWIGGED ON A CONVERSATION BETWEEN MY UNCLE AND HIS FRIENDS. THEY WERE TALKING ABOUT THE NEXT GENERATION OF KIDS FROM CHERNOBYL AND THE POTENTIAL MUTATIONS THAT WOULD OCCUR. I NAIVELY WENT TO BED THAT ENTIRE MONTH DREAMING OF HOW COOL IT WOULD BE TO BE BORN THERE AND I WAS ACTUALLY JEALOUS AT THE THOUGHT OF SOME 'LUCKY' KID BEING THE WORLD'S FIRST REAL SUPERHERO THAT GLOWED IN THE DARK AND WAS A GIANT. AND MY GOD, I FEEL BAD FOR THINKING THAT NOW!

BERLIN WALL
CRASHING DOWN & HASSELHOFF SINGING

I won't say too much about this, because it has to be seen to be believed, so type 'David Hasselhoff Berlin Wall' into YouTube. Picture this: 200,000 'finally free' people on both sides of the Wall at the Brandenburg Gate on New Year's Eve 1989, The Hoff in a black leather jacket with attached lights that flash when he presses a button, standing on a hydraulic lift that brings him 100 feet into the air, a manic booze and/or drug-fuelled grin, a horribly cheesy song about freedom, and two fireworks thrown from the crowd that nearly take his head off. YouTube, quick!!

CHAPTER 13

WHEN...

In the '80s, we were a more innocent people.
Times were simpler, expectation levels weren't so high
and you were just happy with your lot ... FECK THAT!

The '80s were tough in Ireland. There was huge
unemployment, mass emigration and Johnny Logan
was making a nuisance of himself. But here's why we
wouldn't have had it any other way.

WHEN PEOPLE HATED WOODEN FLOORS WITH A PASSION AND THE DREAM WAS TO COVER THE WHOLE HOUSE IN CARPET.

When you would spend evenings making shadow shapes in the candlelight due to the ESB being on strike or just being disconnected.

Sherrrry Christmas Everyobody!

When there was always a bottle of sherry on the sideboard from the previous Christmas.

WAX ON WAX OFF

When you used to karate kick the door shut to avoid letting the heat out of the room.

WHEN EVERYTHING WAS REPAIRED: TVS , WASHING MACHINES, CLOCKS, RADIOS AND BIKES. NOW WE JUST THROW THEM ALL AWAY.

When you would go into the neighbours with your Mammy to make a call before putting money in their little money box beside the phone.

JIM FIXED IT FOR ME

YOU EAT THOSE SPROUTS

When Monday's dinner was always the leftover from Sunday's roast.

When the longest, more worrisome wait was when you were told to,

'WAIT UNTIL YOUR FATHER GETS HOME.'

When your back garden was full of oul' scrap that your grandfather loved.

When you would grow food (spuds and the likes) in your back garden.

When you would head out to catch fish and bring them home to chase girls, squeezing the underbellies to squirt them with fish poo.

When scrapes, grazes, cuts, bruises and concussions were kissed and made better.

STAR

When you thought you were going to be a famous footballer by winning a massive game of World Cup on the green, and when you thought that you were going to be a famous singer by landing the lead solo in your Christmas carol service in school.

When we all thought we dressed well.

WHEN A DOC LEAF WITH SPIT ALWAYS SEEMED TO BE FOUND WHEN STUNG BY A NETTLE

WHEN YOU HATED YOUR OLDER SIBLINGS, BUT KNEW THEY HAD YOUR BACK ON THE ROAD.

SKETCH

When grass whistles were a basic communication tool to warn the gang when parents were approaching, thus allowing time to put the gangs collections of page 3s away.

WHEN THE WORST FEELING IN THE WORLD WAS BEING PICKED LAST FOR A TEAM.

When Houghton stuck it in the English net

DEADLY RAPID DEADLY RAPID

WHEN EVERYTHING WAS 'DEADLY' OR 'RAPID'.

NEW JAMMER

When the sight of a new car on the road would draw a crowd.

When you thought you were minted after making your communion.

NIXERS

ASK A DAD!
NATIONAL SOCIETY OF ODD JOBS

WHEN EVERYONE'S DAD WOULD HAVE A 'NIXER'.

HELP!

When you were asked to 'help the black babies'.

When potential employers would ask a girl to stand up and give them a twirl at an interview.

WHEN YOU LIED ABOUT SINS YOU HAD NEVER COMMITTED AT FIRST CONFESSION.

PRAY

When you would say the Angelus in your Granny's house at 6pm.

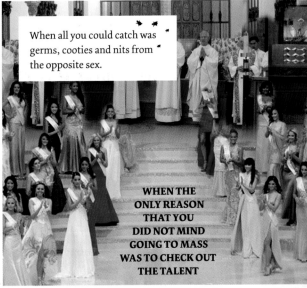

When all you could catch was germs, cooties and nits from the opposite sex.

WHEN THE ONLY REASON THAT YOU DID NOT MIND GOING TO MASS WAS TO CHECK OUT THE TALENT

WHEN TAKING DRUGS MEANT A CAPSULE OF COD LIVER OIL WITH YOUR RICE KRISPIES.

UP THE DUFF

When you would hear about some girl 'who had gotten herself into trouble'.

When your parents told you to leave the room during the *Dallas* episode where the 'poison dwarf' went for an abortion.

When you would hear about Bad Bob's, Club Nassau and Midnight at the Olympia, and could not wait to grow up and go there.

DOUBLE DARE

When you would go carol singing for the local church and then head straight to the chipper with the proceeds.

PLACES YOU'RE NOT ALLOWED GO TO

BAD BOBS
CLUB NASSAU
MIDNIGHT AT THE OLYMPIA

YOU MUST WAIT TO GROW UP!

CHIPPER FUND

When you would have a pen pal.

My time in prison has passed quickly since you have started writing to me. I like meeting older desperate women this way...

WHEN YOU WOULD HAVE CUT OFF YOUR OWN ARM, IF YOU WERE 'DOUBLE DARED'.

When the local GAA team was made up of 16/17 year olds and a bunch of auld fellas due to emigration or worse – working in Dublin.

WHEN YOUR DAD AND UNCLES WOULD MAKE A TRIP TO A COILLTE FOREST IN THE DEAD OF NIGHT IN DECEMBER TO 'BUY' CHRISTMAS TREES FOR THE WHOLE FAMILY.

ELLIS ISLAND

ACKNOWLEDGEMENTS

I have a ridiculous number of people to thank. A few get a mention for heavily influencing me over the years (in good and bad ways!) and a few did feck all, but I said I would give them a name-check for being cheeky enough to ask, 'am I getting a mention?'

I suppose I will start with those who helped me directly with this book. The lads from Red&Grey Design have been immense and I can honestly say that The '80s Kid would not have happened without ye, so thanks a hell of a lot to Bob, Richard, and especially to Keith McGuinness and Killian Walsh. The book would also not have come to pass if it was not for the two girls, Maeve and Stephanie, from Saltwater Publishing. A huge, huge thanks is needed, firstly for taking a punt on me one rainy morning in May. And secondly, for being so fantastic to work with; I wish your new company every success in the future. Much appreciation to Dermot Whelan too! Thanks for coming aboard, for being so positive and encouraging, and for keeping the Big Trak candle burning bright amongst the next generation. Massive gratitude to Louise Whelan (no relation to Dermot!) for endless feedback, encouragement, photography and a lot more, plus extended gratefulness to Louise again, Barry, Nessa and Derek - ye four know why! Big Brian Hegarty (part-time stand-up comedian) also has to get a mention for providing heaps of constructive criticism and info.

And now onto the influences. There are so many: my Granny Rita Murray for being the most amazing lady I have ever met; my Granddad for being an absolute hero; my mother Colette for all the encouragement and for having me in the '80s; Ann, for everything she has done for me; Derek, for pretty much being the Dad I never had; Kim, for buying me heaps of sugary things and for putting up with my crankiness from lack of sleep; Patrick, for 'letting me' practise my Brett 'the Hitman' Hart sharpshooter on

him; and Fiona, Anthony, Maire, Bernadette, Noeleen, Madeline, Pauline and Michael, plus my Godfather Alberto, for treating me like the twelfth child! Every single one of my twenty-two cousins contributed to the madness of my early childhood, especially during the free-for-alls that was Granny's on a Sunday. So mucho thanks to Jennifer, Angela, Paula, Gerald, Barry, Alison, Gary, Louise, David, Anita, Tara, Darren, Emma, Lisa, Sarah, Simon, Jo, Claire, Mickey, Daniel, Mark and my little Goddaughter Katy.

A special thanks to Emma Curley for all she has done for me over the past number of years, for the support during the book and for all her contacts. Big thanks to Emma Keegan for trying your best - you know what I am referring to! More thanks to Audrey and Aisling from The Sweet Emporium on Duke Street, Dublin 2 (they have another shop on Strand Street, Skerries, Co. Dublin), for allowing the shop to be photographed and for housing so many amazing retro sweets that I bring home most Fridays. Even more thanks to everyone who sent me '80s images and to those who kindly gave me permission to use their own personal images when I put them on the spot!

Finally, I must mention the college gang, as they are the source of a few nice stories (don't sue me, lads) contained within the book. T'was a nuts four years and thanks for giving me the full culchie insight to most parts of the country (apologies to the few from the GDA). Thanks to Bonner, Paulie C., Big B., Davy, Byrno, Sarah, Garvey, O'Shea, Reilly, Duignan, Gaughan, Melia (you name-checked me in your thesis), Nicholl, Charlotte, Hayes, Ali, Aine, James Heg, Mac, Lynch, Bolton, Dob, Slow, Caroline, Niamh, Louise, Mooney, Sorcha, etc. (I defo forgot some, sorry!). Plus, thanks to Michelle, Steph and Kevin, and so many others for the little bits of help and encouragement.

WWW.THE80sKID.COM

162